DISCOVER THE WRITER'S LIFE IN NEW YORK CITY.

Over more than six decades of steady innovation, The New School has sustained a vital center for creative writing. The tradition continues with our MFA in Creative Writing, offering concentrations in fiction, poetry, nonfiction, and writing for children. Study writing and literature with The New School's renowned faculty of writers, critics, editors, and publishing professionals. Fellowships and financial aid are available.

FACULTY 2006-2007
Jeffery Renard Allen, Jonathan Ames, Susan Bell, Mark Bibbins, Susan Cheever, Jonathan Dee, Elaine Equi, David Gates, Vivian Gornick, Jennifer Michael Hecht, Shelley Jackson, Zia Jaffrey, Joyce Johnson, Hettie Jones, Deborah Landau, James Lasdun, David Lehman, Suzanne Lessard, Philip Lopate, Honor Moore, Sigrid Nunez, Dale Peck, Robert Polito, Francine Prose, Liam Rector, Helen Schulman, Tor Seidler, Dani Shapiro, Prageeta Sharma, Laurie Sheck, Darcey Steinke, René Steinke, Benjamin Taylor, Abigail Thomas, Paul Violi, Sarah Weeks, Brenda Wineapple, Stephen Wright, and Matthew Zapruder.

VISITING FACULTY
Martin Asher, Joshua Beckman, Frank Bidart, Max Blogg, Deborah Brodie, Patricia Carlin, Emily Fox Gordon, Glen Hartley, Dave Johnson, Rika Lesser, Wendy Lesser, Harry Mathews, Pablo Medina, Sharon Mesmer, Marie Ponsot, David Prete, Matthew Rohrer, Susan Shapiro, Jason Shinder, Ira Silverberg, Frederic Tuten, and Susan Van Metre.

Director: **Robert Polito**

For more information
nsadmissions@newschool.edu
212.229.5630
Visit us online for information session dates

www.writing.newschool.edu

WRITING PROGRAM
THE NEW SCHOOL

An affirmative action/equal opportunity institution

WAR ZONES

7   CONTRIBUTORS

11   **INTRODUCTION**
IAN JACK
the victorious dead

15   **THE LIMEROOM**
JOHN BURNSIDE
fiction

43   **VICTORY IN LEBANON**
WENDELL STEAVENSON
scenes from the hospital corridors

59   **THE COURTHOUSE**
TAHMIMA ANAM
fiction

79   **OPERATION GOMORRAH**
MARIONE INGRAM
a survivor of the Hamburg firestorm

95   **MILITARY LANDSCAPES**
SIMON NORFOLK
picture essay

133   **TOKYO YEAR ZERO**
DAVID PEACE
fiction

GRANTA

157 **THE BASTARD OF ISTANBUL**
ELIF SHAFAK
fiction

175 **TRIDENT**
JAMES BUCHAN
one submarine, 1,500 Hiroshimas

193 **CONGO**
GUY TILLIM
picture essay

213 **THE LITTLE MUSEUM OF MEMORY**
MARK SLOUKA
fiction

227 **THANK GOD WE'VE GOT A NAVY**
BRIAN THOMPSON
how not to be an English officer

243 **LIKE AN EPISODE OF *L.A. LAW***
A. M. HOMES
if only my father was in court

HUMAN RIGHTS WATCH
ON THE BATTLEFIELD AND OFF
WE'RE THERE

DEFENDING HUMAN RIGHTS WORLDWIDE

For the latest news from Human Rights Watch visit: **www.hrw.org**

Above: A child soldier rides back to his base in Congo.
© 2004 Marcus Bleasdale

CONTRIBUTORS

Tahmima Anam was born in Dhaka, Bangladesh in 1975. Her first novel, *A Golden Age* (John Murray), is set against the background of Bangladesh's liberation war of 1971 and will be published in 2007. She lives in London.

James Buchan's most recent book is *Adam Smith and the Pursuit of Perfect Liberty* (Profile) which is published in the US as *The Authentic Adam Smith* (Atlas Books/W. W. Norton). He lives on a farm in Norfolk, England. He last appeared in the magazine with 'This is Centerville' in *Granta* 84.

John Burnside lives in East Fife, Scotland, where he teaches at the University of St Andrews. 'The Limeroom' is taken from his fifth novel, *The Devil's Footprints*. Both the novel and a collection of poems called *Gift Songs* will be published by Jonathan Cape in spring 2007. His non-fiction piece, 'How to Fly', appeared in *Granta* 94.

A. M. Homes is the author of five novels including, most recently, *This Book Will Save Your Life* (Granta Books/Viking), and two short-story collections: *The Safety of Objects* and *Things You Should Know* (Granta/HarperCollins). She is a contributing editor to *Vanity Fair* and teaches at Columbia University. 'Like an Episode of *L. A. Law*' is taken from her memoir, *The Mistress's Daughter*, which will be published by Granta Books in the UK and by Viking in the US in 2007.

Marione Ingram was born in Hamburg in 1935 and today lives in Hamburg and in Washington, DC. 'Operation Gomorrah' is taken from her memoir-in-progress about the Second World War and about her later work as a civil-rights activist in Mississippi. Her fibre art and constructions have been exhibited at galleries in Europe and America.

Simon Norfolk's latest book, *Bleed* (Dewi Lewis), documented war graves in Bosnia. His work was shown in the 2006 Triennial at the International Center of Photography, New York, and will be included in BBC2's six-part history of photography later this year. The essay in this issue is part of a long-term project on war and landscape.

David Peace lives in Tokyo with his wife and two children. He is the author of the *Red Riding Quartet* (Serpent's Tail) and was chosen as one of *Granta*'s Best of Young British Novelists in 2003. His most recent novel is *The Damned Utd* (Faber & Faber). 'Tokyo Year Zero' forms the prologue to his next novel, due to be published later this year, the first in a trilogy which tells the secret history of Tokyo under the American occupation of 1945–52.

Elif Shafak is the author of four novels including *The Gaze* (Marion Boyars). In September 2006 her most recent novel, *The Bastard of Istanbul*, was the first work of fiction to be prosecuted under Article 301 of the Turkish penal code, which prohibits 'public denigration of Turkishness'. She was acquitted. *The Bastard of Istanbul* will be published in the US this spring by Viking.

Mark Slouka is currently Chair of Creative Writing at the University of Chicago. 'The Little Museum of Memory' is taken from his new novel, *The Visible World*, which will be published in spring 2007 by Portobello Books in the UK and by Houghton Mifflin in the US.

Wendell Steavenson has written about Georgia in *Stories I Stole* (Atlantic Books/Grove/Atlantic) and is working on a book about Iraqis. She last appeared in the magazine with 'A Prisoner of the Holy War' in *Granta* 93. She lives in Beirut.

Brian Thompson was born in Lambeth, London in 1935. Since 1973 he has written for radio and television, and worked as a documentary filmmaker. 'Thank God We've Got a Navy' is taken from his second volume of memoirs, *Clever Girl: A Sentimental Education*, which will be published by Atlantic Books in spring 2007.

Guy Tillim's most recent book on Johannesburg (*Jo'burg*, Filigranes Editions) won him the Leica Oskar Barnack Award in 2005. His work has been included in the 7th São Paulo Biennial; in Photography, Video, Mixed Media III in Berlin, 2006; and in iAfrica Remix, which has toured Düsseldorf, London, Paris, Tokyo and Stockholm and arrives at the Johannesburg Art Gallery in February 2007.

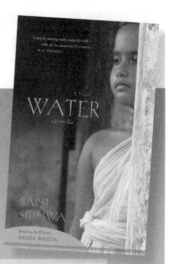

"[A] note-perfect tale of coming of age

in Northern Canada, as beautiful as the landscape is stark."*

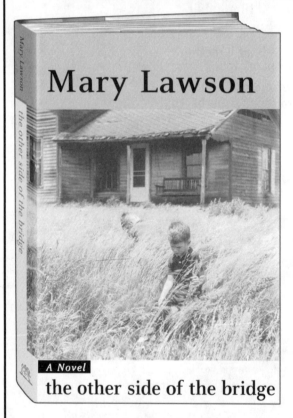

In THE OTHER SIDE OF THE BRIDGE, stolid Arthur and his quicksilver brother Jake's lifelong mutual resentments and betrayals explode in a novel of sibling rivalry, jealousy and obsession, hailed as **"a deftly interwoven story of love and loss"** (*Kirkus Reviews,* Starred Review*).

"In this follow-up to her acclaimed *Crow Lake*, **Lawson again explores the moral quandries of life...**[in] a world...where beauty and harshness are inextricably intertwined." —*Publishers Weekly*

INTRODUCTION

In spite of the cruelty and suffering they inflicted—well known to anyone who fought in one—wars had a remarkably good press among civilians until some years into the twentieth century. In 1914, as the historian Eric Hobsbawm has written, 'the peoples of Europe, for however brief a moment, went lightheartedly to slaughter and to be slaughtered.' There was cheering in the streets of the capitals when war was announced. In Britain, the country which had the strongest political opposition to war, dissent vanished overnight. About 750,000 young Britons volunteered for armed service in the first eight weeks, another million in the next eight months. 'In a way [the war's] coming was widely felt as a release and a relief, especially by the young of the middle classes—men very much more than women—though less so by workers and least by peasants,' Hobsbawm wrote in *The Age of Empire* (1987). 'After a long wait in the auditorium, it meant the opening of the curtain on a great and exciting historical drama in which the audience found itself to be the actors. It meant decision.'

It never happened again. After the First World War, supposedly the war to end all wars, the prospect of armed conflict between nations made people morbid, anxious, and fearful. Ten million dead had knocked sense into them. Five times as many died in the Second World War (including victims of the Holocaust), but few people cheered when it broke out. They knew what they were in for. The mindset of the twentieth century had been set more than twenty years before; a shrunken belief in human progress that, in Hobsbawm's words, predicts 'not a continued ascent, but the possibility, perhaps even the imminence, of some catastrophe: another and more lethal world war, an ecological disaster, a technology whose triumphs may make the world uninhabitable by the human species... We have been taught by the experience of our century to live in the expectation of the apocalypse.'

I don't know how much, if at all, my thirteen-year-old daughter felt about any of this when she went on a school day-trip last summer to the battlefields and memorials of the Somme, just as I have no idea how deeply she and her younger brother were affected by seeing Al Gore's recent documentary about the effects of global warming, *An Inconvenient Truth*. Perhaps both events, one historic and bloody, the other in what may be an even bloodier future, seemed too far away to cause sadness or dread. The Battle of the Somme, which began on July 1, 1916, is as distanced in time from my daughter as the Franco–Prussian war and the Paris Commune, 1870–1871, is from me. When she came back on the school coach to London I asked her how the trip had been and she said that French supermarkets sold pear-flavoured Jaffa Cakes, which are unknown in England. Later she said she had looked for the names of our ancestors on the monuments and found several Gillespies (my mother's name) in the Royal Scots.

Feelings of hate and despair dwindle as they pass down the generations. There were until recently people—usually former inmates of Japanese prison camps, or their relations—who would refuse to buy Japanese cars. My father, who was sixteen when the First World War ended and greatly affected by it, would never wear a red poppy on Armistice Day or drop money into the collecting tin of anyone offering them. The poppies came then from the 'Earl Haig Poppy Factory' and the proceeds went to something called the 'Haig Fund' for wounded servicemen. 'I will never give to anything with that butcher's name on it,' my father would say.

Douglas Haig was the commander-in-chief who on July 1, 1916, ordered British troops on the 'Big Push' forward that became the Battle of the Somme. Many books and a great deal of scholarship have been devoted to the immense tragedy that followed. Perhaps 'callous' and 'incompetent' are the kindest words for Haig, though he wasn't alone among his brother generals in believing that winning the war would mean an unparalleled squandering of human life. The British were to capture German positions on higher ground by the simple expedient of walking in rows—row after row of them—towards enemy machine-guns and barbed wire. More than 19,000 died on that first day, the greatest loss of life in British military history. The stubborn assault went on day after day, week after week, month after month, until by November the British had advanced six miles along a twenty-mile front. In those four months on the Somme, Britain suffered 420,000 casualties, the French 204,000, the Germans 450,000. The German army retook the same ground little more than a year later in 1918.

The Somme wasn't a military turning point in the First World War: the boundary line of the Western Front hardly changed shape and opposing armies went on fighting the trench-war of attrition until the end. But after the Somme it was no longer possible for even the most gullible patriot to regard modern warfare as a brave adventure where death, in the unlikely event it came, would arrive as a nice clean bullet through a cavalry officer's heart. The Somme, as many writers have pointed out, laid the foundations for a new and realistic appreciation of war—the constant cruelty and frequent stupidity of it—that has coloured attitudes ever since.

My daughter's school trip went to the memorial at Thiepval which is dedicated to 'The Missing of the Somme' and built to the design of Edwin Lutyens between 1929 and 1932—the last of the great Western Front memorials to be completed and, according to the architectural historian Gavin Stamp, 'one of the most significant and telling buildings of the last century.' It rises 140-feet tall on a chalk ridge above the river Ancre, a gaunt tower hollowed with arches and tunnels made with a mixture of native French brick and imported Portland stone on which are inscribed the names of 77,357 British soldiers whose remains could never be found or identified.

Like the many other monuments and cemeteries built by the Imperial War Graves Commission, Thiepval doesn't commemorate victory but wasted life, or 'sacrifice' as people at the time needed so badly to believe. As Stamp explains in his excellent history of Thiepval (*The Memorial to the Missing of the Somme*, 2006), this was a relatively new idea in Europe. In the United States, Lincoln had established fourteen national cemeteries for the Union dead immediately after the Civil War, whereas the British dead from Waterloo waited until 1889 before Queen Victoria gave them a monument above their burial ground in Brussels. Until 1918, what Europe liked to monumentalize was victory—the Arc de Triomphe, Nelson's Column—rather than the unlucky, ordinary dead who were scraped together and buried close to where they were found.

The First World War killed the idea of jubilant victory, and though there have been important victories since, most notably in 1945, there have been few victorious monuments. No matter what their outcome, the human cost of wars is what we now choose to remember, as will certainly be the case in Iraq.   *Ian Jack*

GRANTA

THE LIMEROOM
John Burnside

The Limeroom

I live out on the point, at Whitland. It's a lonely spot, I suppose: if you come by car, driving out along the high road, past Seahouses, skirting Sandhaven, then Coldhaven, you come to an odd configuration of telegraph poles, nothing else there but sky and the rise of the hill and, occasionally, the huge flocks of birds that gather, waving and turning in the air like a single fabric of awareness. When you get to the turn-off for Whitland—population today, one—there's nothing; you drive a short distance and all you can see is the cold, grey water of the firth. This is as far east as you can drive; beyond here there's nothing but sheep and buzzards scouting a rocky headland of dune grass and botched gorse and, out on the point, the great colonies of seabirds and wading birds that my father photographed incessantly during his last years. So there are those who would say that this house is isolated—yet it's not far from Coldhaven, if you go on foot. In the house, it feels as if you are high up, especially on the top floor, but it takes only a couple of minutes to follow the little track from our side gate down to Shore Road, and then it's just a few yards to the first houses, on Toll Wynd. Still, it feels comfortably remote, in this era of the car, and it's not visible from anywhere in the town, or from the road for that matter, so it can seem as if I am cut off sometimes. A solitary. A recluse.

My father chose this house. He wanted to be alone, to concentrate on his work. He had come to a point at which he had chosen to live apart; there was a saying he had, a quote from a poem he had read somewhere: 'To be separate, to be apart, is to be whole again.' He had also chosen our first house, on Cockburn Street, but he'd always wanted to be further out, away from people, closer to the birds. He loved the birds here, that was why he came; he loved them more than anything else he knew. They weren't like other life forms to him, they were more an extension of his own mind, his own way of being in the world. He would go out every day with his binoculars and his camera bag and sit on the rocks for hours, but he wasn't really a birdwatcher in the conventional sense; he wasn't a human being observing the gulls and cormorants and wading birds that live around this coast, he was one of them, one of their kind, in his own head, or, rather, in his soul. He was always trying to get me to go out with him, and I'm sorry, now, that I didn't. I was a child, and I was afraid of being seen—afraid, perhaps, of seeing myself—as a birdwatcher, a hobby that was as bad as, or even worse than, stamp collecting or trainspotting. It was fine to collect the cards with pictures of footballers or television stars that came inside those packs of chewing gum they used to sell in The Tuck Shop, it was almost forgivable to collect stamps as a hobby, because you could always say that they were valuable, and you were really doing it for the money, but there was no excuse for birdwatching. Not for a boy.

My first encounter with Malcolm Kennedy was a depressingly predictable affair. I was walking home from school, on a damp, rather wintry afternoon, not long after the Easter holidays. I disliked school, just as I had expected to do, though with a good deal less of the intensity with which I had hated it to begin with. After a while, I think, most children get numbed by school—which is why it's such a good preparation for work—and they sleepwalk through it, learning tables and fragments of grammar by rote. They play games and eat and argue with people they neither like nor dislike, people who could fall down dead at any minute without causing much of a stir—then they go home to do spelling exercises and quadratic equations in little notebooks full of inconsequential comments in red ink from whoever last marked them. That was my experience of the place, anyhow. I minded going; but not enough to take any form of action. Even when Malcolm Kennedy chose me as his special friend, I never once thought of simply staying at home. School was what children did. Adults took photographs and wrote articles, they painted, they chopped up meat and caught fish, they taught mathematics and religious studies. Children went to school so that, one day, they could do the same.

I always walked to and from school alone. I didn't have a best friend, I didn't really have friends at all and, now that we had moved to Whitland, there were no neighbour children to stumble upon by chance along the way. In wet weather, I enjoyed this walk, because my being alone didn't attract attention. When it was dry, however, people would study me as I passed them on the street, trying to remember who I was and giving a half-hearted little scowl, or a knowing smile, when they realized. That day it was damp, and cold, but it wasn't raining, which meant I was walking faster than usual. When it rained I liked to dawdle; I liked how it felt when my school coat, my Burberry, became saturated with water; I liked the feel of the raindrops dripping off my hair and running down my face. Perhaps, if it had been raining that day, Malcolm Kennedy wouldn't have spotted me, and I would never have got to kill anyone.

He was several yards away when he called out. 'Hey,' he cried. 'I *know* you.' I realized he was talking to me almost immediately, but I tried the usual trick of looking the other way, pretending I hadn't registered. 'Hey, *you*,' he called again, louder than before, though he was, by then, almost alongside me. I looked at him. He was tall, bony-looking, a set of odd bulges inside a school uniform and, it seemed, inside his own pelt. It was as if his skeleton was too big for his skin, or maybe he had a few bones too many, an extra elbow here, a surplus shoulder-blade there, all of them vying for space. 'I know you,' he repeated. 'You're Michael Gardiner.'

This was astute of him. We had been going to the same school for six or seven years by then, and he had worked out who I was. I wanted to say as much, but I bit my tongue and nodded.

'You're in Miss Beansmeans class,' he added. Miss Beansmeans was a nickname some of the kids had given Mrs Heinz, a Scotswoman married to a German teacher from another school. I nodded again.

'What's up?' he said, grinning maliciously. 'Cat got your tongue?' *Cat got your tongue* was a favourite expression of Mr Connors, *his* class teacher. Nobody had a nickname for Mr Connors, the man who gave the strap when somebody did wrong in a woman teacher's class. Women weren't allowed to give the strap, a rule that Mrs Heinz, a former athletics champion, greatly regretted.

I didn't know what to say, so I nodded again. This was a mistake, and I realized my error immediately, but Malcolm didn't show the least sign of annoyance. In fact, his grin widened into something beyond a smile, something beyond any other facial expression I'd seen in a human being. His teeth were large; when he grinned, he reminded me of a chimpanzee. Finally, too late, I spoke. 'Yes,' I said.

He laughed. 'Yes?' he said.

I nodded.

'Yes, what?'

I wanted to go. He could see it in my eyes. I wanted to go running home and hide in the little room next to the landing, with my books and records and Airfix kits. When I went out for a walk with my parents, we would sometimes encounter a stray dog, a big, unkempt beast, part-Alsatian, part-something else, that seemed to run wild in the hinterland of dunes and fields above the point. My mother and I were afraid of this dog. When we saw it, she would take my arm, as if to protect me—and maybe that's what she thought she was doing. Naturally, my father's tactic was to ignore the thing. 'Don't be frightened,' he would say. 'Animals can smell fear. It won't do you any harm, unless you provoke it.' I used to wonder how a person could just choose not to be frightened, but I never got round to asking him about it. Now, of course, I knew that I was supposed to *not be frightened* by Malcolm Kennedy—but I didn't know how. I did know, however, that there was enough animal in him to smell my fear. I looked around, hoping for the intervention of some neutral grown-up. There was nobody.

'I like you,' Malcolm said. 'You're smart.' He studied my eyes, still grinning. 'You're a real character,' he said. 'I think we're going to be *special* friends.'

Then he punched me. Not in the face, which was what I was expecting, but on the arm, a sidelong, jabbing punch that hit the bone between the elbow and the shoulder, where it hurts most. I didn't react. I could have hit him back, or run away, but life hadn't prepared me for either of the above, so I just stood there. I think I was waiting for somebody to come and save me.

Malcolm grinned. 'I'll see you later,' he said. He stood watching me for a moment, as if he expected me to reply; when I didn't say anything, his face dimmed and he hit me again: just a tap, a soft, friendly blow. 'All right,' he said. 'Catch you later, sport.' It was something from a book or a comic. Or maybe a film he'd seen on television. He was walking away, hands in his pocket, not looking back at me, and I was thinking: *you got that from a comic, you moron. You can't even think up your own lines.* It was almost funny. 'Catch you later, sport.' Who says something like that? For a moment, I almost felt sorry for him. Then I ran home quickly to the little room next to the landing, so I could make sure my Rupert books were still there, intact.

Bullying takes time, and Malcolm took his time over me, I'll give him that. It must have taken so much energy just keeping track of where I was and when I would be alone, so he could spring his little traps without getting caught out. He was always very quiet-spoken, smiling, almost jovial. He would find me out and make me hand over the money I'd been given for a little snack at break-time, what they called the lief piece. He would walk up to me, hand outstretched, fingers beckoning, and I would just pass the money over. This had to be done quickly, so he wouldn't get caught; all I had to do was hesitate for thirty seconds, for ten seconds, even, and he would have had to slide by, pretending he didn't even know me. But then, I didn't hesitate. As soon as I saw him, I had the money ready, a tight clutch of warm, sweaty coins gathered up in my pocket. Now and then he hit me. He always hit in exactly the same place, between the shoulder and the elbow, on the bone. He was very good at this, as if he'd practised. He didn't do it every time, but he did it enough so I knew who was boss. Sometimes he would take my milk, drink the cream off the top, then hand me back the bottle; other times he would sneak up behind me while I was drinking and jostle me, so the bottle jarred against my teeth, or I spilled the thick, yellowish cream down the front of my jumper. Naturally, I never said a word about any of this to anyone. Nor did I show that I was hurt or upset. I did nothing. I said nothing. Had it not been for an old woman who didn't much like me, to begin with at least, the bullying might have continued all the way through school.

I already knew who she was long before I met her. I'd known about her for years because she was one of the local characters. Her name was Mrs Collings, and why she took up with me is anybody's guess: she had no children of her own; she was lonely, up in her little cottage, half a mile up Clifford Road, between the town and the first strip of farmland; or maybe, as some of the kids in school suggested, she really was a little soft in the head. It didn't really matter, because I didn't choose her, she chose me, and it takes more skill than most children have not to be chosen. Still, it has to be said that our first meeting was fairly inauspicious. It was deep summer and I was off by myself, as usual, wandering the hinterland behind the town. I had come armed with one of the usual instruments of childhood—an old pickle jar from my mother's larder—and I had found a big pool of rosebay willowherb in a dip between the road and the footpath that ran down to the shore. That day, I was being a scientist, a lone scholar of the natural world; when Mrs Collings found me, I was wading through the willowherb, waist deep in flowers and bees, the big pickle jar clasped in my hands, the lid just loose enough that I could lift it quickly when I found a bee at rest on a flower and snap it up. I already had twenty or more of them, a dark cloud of trapped, enraged creatures that rose and fell with every new snap of the lid, droning and throbbing against my right palm like a single crazed entity, but I wanted more—why, I had no idea—and I was still out there, fishing for bees in the heat of a July afternoon when this old woman came by. I immediately froze: I had heard stories at school, and I knew she had a reputation as a crazy person, mean-tempered and unpredictable. I didn't know, then, that she was only a few seasons away from death, or that she had just been told as much, on a visit to the surgery on Shore Street, but I couldn't imagine her wading out there into the undergrowth, if she decided she didn't like the look of me, so I just kept on with what I was doing when she stopped on the path and stood stock-still, glowering. Finally, she spoke. 'How would you like it,' she said, 'if somebody came along and snapped you up in a big jar?'

It wasn't a very original approach, but there was an intensity in her manner that captured my attention—enough, at least, to make me look up. She was pale, almost dead white, yet fierce as a kestrel. I hadn't really seen her before: though I'd passed her on the shorefront a few times, I'd never really stopped to look at her. There was a vagueness about old people, an inbuilt distance, that kept them fairly remote from my child's world; I had no grandparents, and no kindly old neighbours to make a fuss of me, so I had always escaped the attentions of the elderly. That afternoon, however, even at a distance, Mrs Collings was unavoidable. What I saw was a silver-haired woman, brittle and thin as chalk, in a char-grey woollen hat and a Burberry, in spite of the heat; she was taller than I expected, and nowhere near as old, though she looked tired and weak, with that air people have when they are ill of having to make an effort just to stay upright. It was her face, though, that held me: a face drained of colour and substance, but alight with righteous indignation, for these bees, and for all the helpless creatures of the earth. 'Well?' she said. 'Cat got your tongue?'

As it happened, the cat, or something, *had* got my tongue. I couldn't think of a word to say; or rather, I suddenly had a great deal to say, but I didn't know how to say it. It had never occurred to me, before, to tell a grown-up about Malcolm Kennedy; now, faced with this fiery old woman, who sounded just like him, I wanted to let it all come tumbling out, the whole story, in all its ugly little details. But I couldn't;

not then. I was afraid of her, a little; and I was fascinated, a little; but mostly I was just taken aback that she had even noticed me. 'I'm going to let them go,' I ventured, after a long pause for thought.

'Aha.' She shook her head sadly; then she gave me a tight little smile. 'And how are you going to do that?' she asked.

I stared at her. I had no idea; yet I had planned to let the bees go, because I wasn't the malicious little boy she thought I was, I was a scientist, a dispassionate observer of the natural world. What I was after was knowledge, not cruelty. But then, how did you release twenty or so bees from a jar. 'I don't know,' I said. I think I was hoping she would tell me.

'Well,' she replied, softening. 'Try not to get stung to death, won't you?' And without a second glance, she walked on.

That was the total extent of our first encounter and I imagine, from her point of view, there was nothing more to be said. For me, though, it was only a beginning. I tried, of course, to shrug the whole thing off: just some nosy old bag, who did she think she was anyway? That kind of thing. Then I proceeded to think about her all afternoon, trying to build a complete picture from the few scraps I'd heard in passing: she had once owned the florist's shop on Shore Street, but she had sold it and gone to live by herself in an old cottage up by Ceres after her husband died. Some people said she was rich, and she had piles of money hidden somewhere in her house; others said she was a witch. I knew this was nonsense, of course.

Before I met Malcolm Kennedy, I thought I knew about fear. It was a phantom, out in the woods; or it lived in the old limeroom, a mummified creature wrapped in cold rags, soot-stained, raw, decaying slowly under broken strip lights. Or maybe it wasn't decaying, maybe it was returning, like Lazarus. Maybe it was changing: a man in the process of becoming a bird, or a bird that had started to become a man, hideously ugly, perhaps, but capable of inspiring pity, making its nest in the roof beams, cut off from others of its kind until the transformation was complete. I had read too many comic books, and I had seen too many films; that was why I could imagine fear in such a guise, and that was why I could flirt with it, wandering out along the old railway tracks on a summer's day, or sitting up in the limeroom, under the dark trees, watching for the phantom. That was why I was so numb when Malcolm Kennedy chose me to be his special friend. I had wanted fear to be more beautiful, I had wanted it to be more thrilling. I could hardly bear it that it was so ordinary.

And that it endured. Most days, it was the same routine, and I was as bored with it as I was scared and angry. Now and again, though, he came up with something new, some plan he had been nurturing for a while, waiting for an opportunity to put it into action. Usually, it was just him, which was scary enough, but one afternoon—a Saturday, as I recall—there was another boy, someone I had seen before but didn't know by name. I had been up at the limeroom, idling away the afternoon under the trees, when the two boys appeared in my path, cutting me off from Whitland, and safety. I didn't know what to do—because, of course, there was nothing I *could* do—so I kept on walking, just going about my business, hoping they would let me brazen it out. I knew the worst thing would be to run; odd as it seems, any attempt to escape would have been an admission of something— an admission of guilt, an admission that I deserved what was coming—as well as an insult to my special friend. The main thing was to show that he had the power, always, and that I accepted this as only right and proper. By continuing to walk homeward, head down, not looking at them, I imagined that things could be left open, and Malcolm Kennedy had the opportunity, if he chose, to be lenient.

'Hey! You!' It was the other boy who called me. There was no real need, he was only a few yards away, but he called out anyway, so I would have to look up at him. Or maybe it was just for the pleasure of hearing his voice ring out in the still summer air. 'Hey, kid! Where you going?'

I looked up. The other boy was a little too fat, but he was stocky with it, and he looked mean.

'You deaf?' the boy said. They were standing in front of me now, blocking my way.

'I'm going home,' I said, trying not to sound defiant, trying not to sound scared.

The boy laughed. 'Oh no, you're not,' he said. 'You're not going home. Is he, Malkie?'

I looked at Malcolm Kennedy. He seemed serious, thinking about something that was his alone to think about. Finally, he spoke; but not to me. 'Shut up, Des,' he said. 'You're getting on my nerves.'

He looked at me. 'Don't worry about Des,' he said. 'He's just rude. You know. Uncouth.' He smiled. 'What Des actually means is, we'd like you to come out to the loch with us. Don't you, Des?' Des didn't say anything. He was sulking. 'I said,' Malcolm Kennedy repeated, an edge of firmness in his voice, 'don't you, Des?'

Des nodded unhappily, and shot me an angry glance. 'We'd like you to come out to the loch with us,' he said, almost but not quite in a mocking singsong.

'So,' Malcolm Kennedy said, looking suddenly cheerful again. 'Are you coming? We can't stand here all day.'

'I've got to get home,' I said. 'My Dad—'

Malcolm smiled sweetly. 'You won't be late,' he said. 'We'll see you get home all right. Won't we, Des?'

Des nodded. 'Oh yes,' he said. 'We'll see you get home all right.'

It was fast coming on for that grey, slightly sooty time of the evening, when the distance looks lighter and closer than the ground beneath your feet. We had gone down the dirt track that ran east, then north, where the Seahouses road gave out; then we had followed a sticky black footpath into the stretch of marshy land beyond, a place my father loved, for the birds he found there. At one point we had even passed within sight of our house, and I thought again about running, but I knew there was no point. Des walked on ahead, with a stick in his hand, slashing and flailing at the plants on either side of the path, while I walked silently alongside Malcolm Kennedy, my mind racing, wondering what fresh humiliation was in store. It was damp underfoot here, a little sticky, but the sky above us was clear. Finally, we had come to a sludgy area of reeds and water that some people called the loch, though it was really just wet marsh surrounded by squat birch trees and willow, a little pocket of it, within a mile or so of the seashore. 'This is the place,' Malcolm Kennedy had announced, and we'd stopped walking.

Now they were looking for nests in the wet patches at the edge of the loch, moorhens' or coots' nests that, out here, were fairly easy to find. I remembered, then, that Malcolm Kennedy had a collection of birds' eggs, a collection of which he was proud enough to have brought into school to show off at parents' day. I remembered seeing it: several shortbread tins full of brown and cream and blue eggs, all of them cold and empty, a little white ticket alongside each one, with the name of the bird written out in surprisingly fine calligraphy. The teachers hadn't much approved of that, but he'd said it was an old collection that his dad had given him, and that he didn't go out nesting himself, so they had let him bring it in. I imagine, looking back, that they were just trying to find some way to encourage a boy who otherwise showed no interest in anything. Of course, he did go nesting, but this wasn't the right time of year; now there wouldn't be any eggs, just empty nests and little broods of chicks, out on the water. I began to panic. I had been afraid before, but it had all turned out to be fairly ordinary, three boys taking a walk in the countryside on a Saturday afternoon, and I'd got my hopes up. Now, I realized that something bad was going to happen.

All of a sudden, Malcolm Kennedy stopped; then, looking down into the water, he raised his hand. 'Look!' he said.

I looked, but Des didn't seem interested. It was a family of moorhens, the mother and about eight chicks, paddling around in a little pool of dark, sooty-looking water. The mother seemed alarmed, and swam between us and her brood making an odd, almost conversational piping sound that presumably signalled danger. The chicks stayed close.

Suddenly, Malcolm Kennedy exploded into movement, splashing into the water, scattering the mother and her brood and grabbing at something. At first I thought he'd seen a fish, and was trying to catch it; then I realized what he was up to. Des came over and stood beside me at the edge of the water. He looked mildly interested now, recovered from his sulk. 'Come on, Malcolm,' he said. 'Come on.'

After several minutes of scrambling and splashing around, Malcolm Kennedy emerged from the water. He was holding something in his cupped hands. 'Got it,' he said. He looked at me. His face was wet, his hair was dripping water. 'You want to see it?' he asked.

Des sidled forward, trying to see the catch. Behind us, in the first grey of the twilight, the mother moorhen was calling again, bringing her chicks together, checking to see if they were all there. I assumed she would find one missing. Des moved closer.

'Not you, fucker,' Malcolm Kennedy said, his voice ugly. '*Him.*' He held out the bony cage of fingers and knuckles, right in front of my face.

I shook my head. 'I don't want it,' I said.

'No?'

'No.'

'But I just caught it for you.'

'No.'

'Really?'

I nodded.

'Go on. It's for you.'

I shook my head. I didn't want to kill anything, and I knew that *that* was what it was coming to.

Malcolm Kennedy looked disappointed. Then, without taking his eyes off me, he opened his hands. The chick fell to the ground and started fluttering about madly, but before it could get away, he looked down, made out where it was in the summer gloaming and, silently, calmly, in no particular hurry, he crushed it underfoot.

'Bugger me,' he said. 'Now look what you made me do.'

That was enough. I knew it was over, that he'd done what he wanted to do. As he ground the chick into the mud and rushes, I turned tail and ran for it, splashing through water and mud, losing the path and finding it again, aware of nothing but the sound of my own breathing, till I reached the road and slowed to a halt, gasping for air. There was no traffic, no noise. I crossed the road and started down the track to Whitland, noticing as I went how dirty and wet I was, all spattered with mud and marsh water. I was late, my parents would want an explanation; I didn't know what I would say. All I knew was, I couldn't tell the truth. I knew it would have hurt my father too much, though I didn't really know why.

It was Malcolm Kennedy who introduced me to Mrs Collings again, in a roundabout way. It happened on a Wednesday, an hour after school; I know it was a Wednesday because I had been to my piano lesson. I was feeling good that afternoon, till Malcolm Kennedy caught me on the shore road, not fifty yards from home. Nobody else was around, but I could see the end of the track that ran up to Whitland, and it made me angry, that he had deliberately waited till I was almost home, before catching me up. Since the episode out on the marshes, he had kept his distance, just darting in every now and then, in the playground, or when I was walking home, to mutter some dark warning, not hitting me, hardly stopping, but promising that

27

John Burnside

something bad was coming to me, threatening to kill me, sometimes in words that were murmured so quickly and quietly that I couldn't make out what he was saying. What I could make out, though, was the depth of his malice towards me. He was angry; he was determined to do me real harm. I knew it. He was waiting for his moment and, in the meantime, he was enjoying the simple pleasure of watching me suffer. He didn't need to hit me, he *had* me already—and he knew it.

'*You're dead, Gardiner.*'

'*I'm going to get you, Gardiner. That's not a threat. It's a promise.*'

'*What is it, Mikey? You scared?*' A big, toothy smile, like the Crimson Pirate. '*You'd better be.*'

Now, he'd caught me where nobody could see us, just yards from home, and I knew the time had come for him to make good on his promises. 'Hey,' he said. '*Mi*key.' He had taken to calling me Mikey over the last few weeks.

I turned. There he was, in his school clothes, all bone and angle, a big smile on his face. I didn't say anything; there was no point.

'Well, aren't you going to say hello?' he asked.

I thought about making a run for it. There was something in his manner, an exaggerated lightness of mood, that scared me. Today was going to be special. But then, if I ran, he would catch me. He was bigger, and he was always ready, always prepared. Really, he should have been a Boy Scout. He could see in my eyes what I was going to do before I did it; he could see, at that very moment, that I was thinking of running, and his tongue flickered between his lips in soft appraisal, as if he too were working out the odds that were going through my head. I crumpled. 'Hello,' I said.

'That's better.' He beamed. 'Now, come along with me, Mikey. There's a little experiment I want to try.'

He turned and led the way back down the rise, knowing I wouldn't try to escape. When we got to Toll Wynd, he cut in behind the first two houses, and led me through a narrow, almost impassable alleyway that I didn't even know existed until that moment. It was dank and stony and smelled of pee. There were dead things in there, and tangles of old clothes amidst the broken crates and litter, all of it saturated with months of dirt and rain, but half dried out now, rank and matted underfoot, like walking on mouldy leaves, or mouldy flesh. Up ahead, Malcolm Kennedy gave an odd little snicker.

'Rats in here, I shouldn't wonder,' he said. 'Big fat ones.' He glanced back at me. 'Snakes, maybe,' he said. 'You like snakes, Mikey?'

I didn't answer. He turned away, snickering, and I followed. Finally, we emerged into the smallest courtyard I had ever seen. At one time, it would have been overlooked by the first house on Toll Wynd, but the lower windows at the back of the building had been bricked up. To the rear of the house, a low, sandstone outhouse stood disused, its door hanging open. Then I remembered: at one time, there had been a dairy here, but it had closed long ago, and now only the front of the house, where the little shop had been, was still in use. The man who lived there, an ancient creature with the most astonishing goitre, restricted himself to the front room and the kitchen, both of which looked out on to the street. Here, it was just outbuildings and an old outside toilet, its green cistern crumbling on the wall, the rust stains dry now, but still dark, like freshly healed wounds. I looked at Malcolm. I just wanted it, whatever it was that he had in mind, to be over.

'Do you know where we are?' he said.

I nodded. 'It's the old dairy,' I said.

'So it is.' His face darkened suddenly. 'Take your jumper off,' he said.

'What?'

'You heard me.'

'No.'

He stepped forward and punched me in the face. I tried to back away and he grabbed me. 'Take you jumper off,' he said again, really angry now, but still quiet.

I pulled free and stood, watching him. He was calm again, confident, still in control. The tears were coming now. I was terrified. I thought he had a secret hoard of rats in there, rats, or snakes and he wanted to feed me to them. I thought he was going to do something unspeakable, something I couldn't even have imagined. I shook my head desperately, and I felt my bottom lip go. It was the first time I had really cried in front of him. He'd made my eyes smart, he'd brought me to the point of tears, but I'd never actually blubbered in his presence.

'Take your jumper off,' he said again, quietly. I kept shaking my head, trying to figure out what was happening, sobbing with fear.

He could punch me all he liked, but he wasn't going to feed me to the rats. Snot was running out of my nose, the tears were streaming down my face.

He looked down, as if considering. 'All right,' he said after a moment. 'Suit yourself.'

He ran at me then and barged me to the ground. I fell hard, straight on my back, and I heard a damp, muffled sound: the thud of myself falling. Shoulders, back, spine, lungs, ribs. He had winded me. I couldn't breathe, couldn't see, couldn't think. I just lay still, in an airless, bluish place, while Malcolm Kennedy got to his feet and leaned in over me, an invisible, breathing presence. He was immense.

I dream of him now, sometimes. Not often, and mostly as he was on that last day, treading water in the limeroom and calling out for help; sometimes, though, I see him as he looked that summer's afternoon, taller and broader and darker than he really was, an immensity, a demigod. I bestow upon this dream creature, this counterfeit, a gravity he never had in life, and then I wake to moonlight over the firth, or to the dawn birds, and I am glad to be alive; and I am glad that he is dead. That gladness is also immense, bigger than anything else I have ever experienced. It is as if the world had been waiting years to happen, waiting patiently through terror and grief and the weight of myself.

What happened next, I didn't really see or hear. I was still winded, still dizzy, coming back from the blue; only now I felt sick, and cold in my head, and I wanted to vomit.

'Hello?' It was another voice. A woman's voice. An old voice. '*Hello?*' She was standing over me, a thin, elderly woman in a blue coat, her face white, her mouth very red: Mrs Collings. For a moment, I was shocked: how had she come to be there? I struggled to my feet.

'Who was that boy?' she asked.

I didn't answer. I don't think she expected me to. I put my hand to my face. Something was happening, but I wasn't sure what: there was something sweet and wet in my nose, and I felt dizzy; it took me a moment to work out that I had a nosebleed. It wasn't the fall that had caused it, it was just the fear, and she knew it as well as I did. She reached into her coat pocket and pulled out a tiny, neatly folded handkerchief, embroidered at the edges with red and blue flowers.

'Here,' she said. 'Your nose is bleeding.'

I nodded. I didn't really want to take her hankie, it was so white, and so very small.

'Come on,' she said. 'I've got others.'

I took the handkerchief and pressed it to my nose.

'Put your head back,' she said.

I tipped my head back with the hankie still pressed to my nose. I could feel the blood running back into my throat and sinuses. I imagined it running into my ears.

'Stand like that a minute,' she said. 'Head back. Very still. You'll be fine in no time.'

The following Saturday, I climbed the rise up to Ceres cottage to return her hankie. I had told my mother about the nosebleed and about Mrs Collings, but not about Malcolm Kennedy. She had said she knew how to get the blood out, and she had washed and ironed it so that it looked as good as new, folding it as it had been when Mrs Collings gave it to me, a little square of linen with the embroidered roses showing. Then she told me I had to return it to Mrs Collings and I had gone, my curiosity just strong enough to overcome my nervousness. It was another warm day, but the sky was overcast by the time I reached the cottage. I knocked. At first nobody answered, and I thought about giving up; then Mrs Collings appeared, her hands grimy, her hair a little untidy. She looked at me, then at the hankie.

'You brought it back,' she said. 'How considerate.'

'My mum washed it,' I said.

'So I see.' She took the hankie from my outstretched hand and studied it. 'And a very good job she did, too. Couldn't have done it better myself.' I had no answer for this, if it required an answer, so I said nothing. I wondered if it would be rude to go. Then I wondered if it would be rude not to. She put the handkerchief in her pocket; then she looked at me curiously. 'I suppose you'll want to come in for some cake,' she said. 'That's what old ladies do, isn't it? Make cakes all day, in case some hungry boy comes a-calling?'

I nodded, and she laughed. That was the beginning of our friendship, though I'm not sure that friendship is exactly the word. Which is to say, I'm not sure if she wanted to be friends with *me*, as such. She was always kind to me and she did, in fact, make cakes every time I came to visit. Still, I couldn't quite shake off the thought that what she was really interested in was my predicament with Malcolm Kennedy; she was old, and she was dying, and I think she wanted one last fight before she died. Not that I knew any of this at the time. At the time, I was flattered that she invited me to come again—very formally, with an odd little bow of the head—each time I went to visit. I was pleased to have someone to talk to about the things I didn't discuss with my parents and, though she didn't pursue the matter, I knew it was only a matter of time before she told me what I needed to do to escape the attentions of Malcolm Kennedy. I don't know how I knew this, but I was *sure* of it: she had an answer, and all that was needed was for me to show, in some way that I still couldn't guess, that I was ready to hear it.

Meanwhile, she talked about her life. She told me how she had bought the florist's shop—it had been a bakery at one time, then a greengrocer's—more or less on a whim, because she had the money and the time to do it, and because she loved flowers. 'Even if you don't need any flowers,' she said, 'you should go into a florist's every now and then, on Valentine's Day, for instance, just to see all that colour—all that crimson and damask and rose-pink.' She looked at me wistfully. 'Colour is good for the soul, boy,' she said. 'Remember that, when you're grown. Buy flowers now and again, it will do you good. Don't buy them for your girlfriend, buy them for yourself.' I winced at the idea of a girlfriend, but I managed a nod, and I remembered this, along with all the other pieces of advice she gave me. I kept them in my head and turned them over from time to time, wondering if they were true, or right. To some extent, I suppose I lived by them.

One day, with no particular fuss or fanfare, Mrs Collings began to talk to me about Malcolm Kennedy. By that time, she had found out who he was, who his parents were, what they did, who they were related to, all the things that matter in a small town. She didn't say much at first, she didn't really say that much at any one time, she mostly insinuated. She told me I wasn't really afraid of Malcolm Kennedy; I was afraid of myself. I was afraid of doing something final, afraid of acting. Most people are, she said. We turn our heads and look the other way, or we suffer for a while, so we don't have to do anything decisive. Because it's *doing something*—it's ourselves acting—that frightens us. And the thing to do with fear is to change it. You can't avoid it; you can't get rid of it; you can't throw it away. So you have to use it. You have to change it. If you need a weapon, it becomes a weapon. If you need a shelter, it can become a shelter—but, first, it has to be changed. That was all she taught me. Change your fear into something else. Righteous anger. Compassion. Fighting spirit. You can even make it into love, with enough work. That was Mrs Collings's lesson to me. I had to change my fear into what I needed most, and what I needed, at that particular moment, was cunning. A cunning person can become invisible, if he tries. He can become the hunter, not the hunted. If Malcolm Kennedy was tracking me all the time, I had to become invisible—and then I had to start tracking him. 'If you have an enemy,' she said, 'the first thing you have to do is get to know him. You have to know how he thinks and what he knows and, most of all, what he wants. Because what he wants is where he is weak.' Or she would say, 'It's not him you need to change, it's yourself. You have to stop caring, you have to learn to be patient. Bide your time, that's the secret. *Bide your time.*'

I'm not saying she always said as much as this, in so many words. Sometimes, she told me stories, little parables of fear and cunning. She told me how the Samurai warriors would prepare for battle by deciding that they were dead already and so had nothing to lose. She told me about the Stoics, who freed themselves from mental and physical slavery by a sheer effort of logic. It wasn't so much a case of her telling me what to do, or teaching me about myself and the world around me, as an old woman telling stories to a twelve year old. Still, for a long time, I dismissed what she was saying. It was easy for her to talk about fear and cunning and being invisible, I thought, sitting there by the fire. But how was I supposed to become invisible? How was I supposed to become cunning? It was all just fancy talk, I told myself. It was like my father telling my mother and me not to be afraid when we met the dog on our Sunday walks. You were either afraid or you weren't, you couldn't control it. Besides, being afraid was a good idea, sometimes. Maybe most of the time. Being afraid was a pretty good preparation for the world, as far as I could see. Better, anyhow, than being stupid and just rushing into things.

And then, one day, all at once, I understood. I had been getting it wrong all that time because, to defeat Malcolm Kennedy, I had imagined I had to *be* like him, only more so. I had to be as big, then bigger, as cruel, then crueller, as strong, then stronger. Which was impossible, because I wasn't like him at all. Now, however, I saw that this was my big advantage. Now I could see that, to defeat him, I had to find the one way in which he was like me, the connection, the way in. I had to find the part of him that didn't want to be a forlorn child in a narrow seaside town, a boy among grim-faced adults whose only life was church and work, a boy who dreamed of getting away, of being elsewhere—in Tierra del Fuego, say, or crossing the Great Plains on horseback, alone in the world, under a wide sky. A boy who could be snared, from time to time, by a wisp of perfume when Miss Pryor leaned over his desk and, dizzy with a longing he didn't even begin to understand, forgets who he is supposed to be and exists only as desire. The boy he must have been, sometimes, when there was nobody to bully, a boy walking along a beach on a summer's afternoon. A boy capable of happiness; a boy capable of weakness. Of course, I couldn't have thought about it in these terms then, but I understood. I *understood*.

Mrs Collings noticed the change. 'Good,' she said. 'Now you're ready. Give yourself eleven days. Become invisible. Watch him. Find out who he is. See through him.'

I nodded. I was excited; I really did think it would work. The trouble was, I didn't stop to think about what Mrs Collings might want me to do. And maybe she didn't either. Which is a common enough problem, I suppose. It's all very well when the downtrodden and the victimized win back some kind of power, but the real trick is in knowing how to use it. Most of the time, I suspect, the easiest thing to do is just to turn it against oneself, and the only question that remains is how directly, or how indirectly, this is done. It's never really a decision, this seizing of power; it's more a sense of the inevitable, a sense of arrival. The moment arrives and it seems possible, even necessary, to act and, without really choosing to do it, we act. We do what we cannot avoid doing.

I learned to be invisible in those eleven days when I was observing Malcolm Kennedy. Really. It was easier than I had expected, too; though, looking back, I can see that Malcolm Kennedy didn't know I was watching him because that was the last thing he would have imagined me doing. Why would I be following him around, watching his every move, risking another of his attacks? Why would I risk losing my supposed status of special friend and so become an outright enemy? He had no reason to suspect that the tables had been turned, because it was something that would never have occurred to him—and because he knew it was something that would never have occurred to me either. Still, I was surprised by my own patience and by my ability to stay hidden and watchful at the same time. I kept thinking of what Mrs Collings had told me. *Bide your time.* That was the secret. There was something very satisfying about that phrase. I was discovering this deep reserve of patience I never knew I had, and I was surprised at how rich it was. For eleven days, I observed him the way a field worker or a wildlife cameraman observes a dangerous animal, with all due caution, but also with a certain dispassion, without the fear, or the awe, or even the pity that had trapped me till then. For months I had wondered at the sheer single-mindedness, the sheer inventiveness of his malevolence. For months, he had been the hunter, and I had been the prey. Now I became quiet, still, self-contained. I was learning him, just as Mrs Collings had told me to do. *Watch him,* she had said. *Get to know him. See how small he is. Find his weaknesses.* Finally, I was ready to act. I had my plan; I had gone over it carefully; it wasn't necessarily foolproof, but it had a surface innocence that appealed to what Mrs Collings had called my inner chess player.

It was a Friday afternoon, right after school. Most days, I now knew, Malcolm Kennedy hung around the gate after school, or he would wander home slowly, going the long way round, looking in shop windows, or standing outside the old library, killing time. It took me a few days to figure out why; then I remembered somebody saying that his mother worked late at the Spar, and I realized he couldn't go home, because he didn't have a key. He walked around in town, trying to stay warm, his hands in his pockets, his face reddening from the cold. He had his favourite stopping places: Mackie's, with its display of sheath knives and fishing gear, set right out alongside the lengths of copper tubing and dreening rods in the window; Henderson's, where they made those tiny, American-style doughnuts I liked, the ones that were all covered with sugar.

That day, though, I had a surprise for him. He hadn't seen me for so long, I think it took him aback when I suddenly appeared in his path, aware of him—*waiting* for him. Before he could speak, I walked up to him.

'You'll never guess what I saw,' I said, all breathless and propitiatory. 'It's amazing. You never get them round here, but my dad saw it, and he showed me where it was—'

'What are you talking about?' he said, annoyed. The spell wasn't working. He'd probably been about to hit me, just to shut me up and regain control of the situation, but there we were, right on Shore Street, with maybe teachers going by on their way home—and now, suddenly, I was offering him something. For the moment, at least, I had his attention.

'The icterine warbler,' I said. 'You read about it in the papers, didn't you? It's almost unknown—'

His left hand flared out, but he didn't make contact. 'Wait a minute,' he said. 'Slow down. Calm down.' He'd got that from television too. 'Where did you say you saw it?'

I grinned; naive, trusting, hopeful. 'I'll show you,' I said.

He regarded me with natural suspicion. Why would I want to do that? But then—what harm could it do? I was no danger to him, not a little pipsqueak like me. What was I going to do, set a trap for him? It was ridiculous. I could see the wheels turning. 'All right,' he said. 'But you better be right. I got better things to do with my time than run off on any darned wild-goose chases.'

I smiled happily. I had to hand it to him, this guy watched a lot of TV. 'It's this way,' I said, with real and feigned excitement. Now that it was all set in motion, I was hardly scared at all. 'Follow me,' I said.

He was sceptical, still, but he couldn't resist the temptation. He had nothing to be frightened of. And if I was lying to him, he had a perfect excuse to really go to work on me. A risk I knew I was taking, of course. But I was excited. I was ready. I knew him, I had observed him, and I knew he was smaller in real life than I had ever imagined. So I led the way. I tricked him. I took him to the old limeroom.

The limeroom was an old stone building on the edge of a strip of farmland, just above the town. It had been abandoned for years; the roof was damaged and inside there were two long, deep pits full of black, viscous-looking water. It smelled of diesel and old sacking and animals and rot, but most of all, it smelled of lime. At the dark end, about thirty feet from the door, a row of galvanized iron troughs stood against the wall, full of cobwebs and dust and traces of leaf slime. I used to go there in the summer and sit around in the shade, doing nothing, just listening to the birds in the trees overhead, or the rain dripping off the boughs on to the roof. Nobody else attached any importance to the place; nobody ever went there. Even the name, the limeroom, was a private one that I had given it. I suppose other people saw it as some old farm building, but I thought it was the holy ground itself. On summer mornings, I would go out there early on my bike and watch the dawn from the half-open doorway. In that corner of the fields, the sun came up through the trees, instead of over the water, and it looked completely different from the point, or the promenade. Sometimes it came up almost white and ghostly, and you had to look hard for it, through the leaves; other times, especially in early spring, it seemed to come bouncing off the horizon like a big red ball, suffusing the bare trees with wet, crimson fire.

I had chosen that place because it was lonely, and because I thought it would bring me luck. Sometimes places bring you luck, if you know them well enough. I chose the far corner of the building, above the long, deep pit of black, rank water, for the icterine warbler's nesting place. I knew nothing about birds in those days, though I should have been an expert. My father just couldn't understand it, that I didn't want to go out birdwatching with him. He even bought me my own binoculars, to encourage me, but I still couldn't bring myself to. And I really did regret that, after he died. He loved birds so much, and he knew about them all, about their habits and their calls and where they liked to nest. Naturally, I had no idea where an icterine warbler usually sought shelter—probably not in a dank old building—but then, since they were birds that didn't normally nest in Britain, I didn't imagine Malcolm Kennedy would know any better. He wasn't a birdwatcher, anyway. He didn't even like birds. He just wanted to add another egg to his collection. Still, one problem remained. I had got him to the limeroom, now I had to get him into that dark, dangerous corner, without seeming to be up to anything. I had to be cunning. I had to deceive him.

'God, it stinks in here,' he said, as we slipped through the half-open door. 'What is this place?'

I shrugged. 'I don't know,' I said. 'Just an old farm building, I think.'

He stood in the half-gloom of the interior, looking around. 'What's that big pit for?' he said.

'I don't know.' I advanced towards the back of the building. 'You stay here,' I said, starting towards the narrow ledge, a ledge about two inches wide, that ran along the back of the wall, overhanging the pit. I had crossed it once, safely, one afternoon—but then I had been on my own, with nothing to distract me. 'I'm going over to the other side. That's where the nest is.'

He grabbed my sleeve. 'What do you mean *you're* going over,' he said. '*I'm* going over.' He peered up into the darkness. 'Where is this nest, anyway?'

'It's all right,' I said, trying to free myself. 'I know exactly where it is. And I know how to get across. It's very narrow—'

He pulled me back again. '*I'm* going,' he said. 'Just tell me where the nest is.'

It appeared then that, with some reluctance, and feeling cheated yet again, I gave in. 'All right,' I said. 'But watch your step. It's very—'

'You said,' he almost snarled. 'Where's the fucking nest?'

I pointed up into the corner. 'See there,' I said. 'Where that dark stain is? There's a little gap, just above. You can't see it from here, but you can feel it. That's where the nest is.'

He looked up. He could only reach the gap—there really was a gap there, I had seen birds flying into it, once—by standing on tiptoe. That would be when he was most vulnerable. Standing on tiptoe, with his arm stretched as far as it would go, trying to feel where the nest was, trying to find the eggs—that was when he would fall. All he needed was a little help. At the time, I had no intention of doing him any permanent harm. I just wanted him to fall into that dark, greasy water and flail around for a while, wallowing in the muck. It would be him, this time, who would be humiliated; it would him who looked like a fool. He would know I had tricked him, and if I could trick him once, if I could get the upper hand once, I could do it again. I wasn't afraid— or I wasn't as afraid as I'd thought I would be. I was perfectly focused on the image of him in the pit, treading water, calling out for help. Help that only I could offer. And I would refuse. I would laugh at him and walk out into the fresh air and leave him there, floundering.

He took a moment to get his bearings, to fix in his mind the place where the supposed nest was; then he set off. He was pretty agile, edging along, his back to the wall, using it to balance as he went, carefully, not hurrying, but not overcautious either. He took his time, but then I think he was also showing off a little. He wanted me to see that he could do it, better than I ever could, probably; he wanted me to take back what I had said about how narrow it was, and how difficult it would be. Slowly, his face set in concentration, he edged his way across. Soon he was close. 'You're almost there,' I said, a little too loudly. I wanted him to think I was encouraging him. I was exactly where he wanted me, servile, obsequious, the dumbstruck witness of his superior boyhood. The trouble was, I startled him a little, and he wobbled, just perceptibly.

'All right,' he said. 'No need to shout. You'll disturb the birds.'

I nodded stupidly. 'Sorry,' I called, not quite as loudly.

He looked back at me and grimaced. 'All right,' he said. 'Am I there now?'

'Yes,' I shouted. 'You're right below it. If you turn around and put your left hand up, you'll find the gap.'

'Will you stop fucking shouting,' he shouted. 'I'm trying to concentrate here.' He turned carefully, shuffling his feet in tiny steps like a dancer, till he had his back to me. He was right in the far corner, pressed against the wall. He lifted his left arm and started feeling about above him. 'I can't find it,' he said. 'Are you sure—'

'A little to the left,' I called, as I fetched the pole. It was something I had found on the waste ground next to the limeroom, a long wooden pole, a little like a clothes prop, but without the V-shaped nick at the end. I had no idea what it had been used for, before it was abandoned there, but I had a use for it now. Because he wasn't looking back, and he was stretching as far as he could, and he was preoccupied with something, an avid child, with his mind set on what he was going to get out of this day's business, he was an easy target. I had rehearsed it any number of times, in my mind, and in that dark corner of the real world, and I knew it was possible, with some luck, and more judgement and, most of all, resolve. I had to steel myself. I had to stop being afraid. Now I knew what my father meant when we met that stray dog on our walks. 'Don't be afraid,' he had said. Now I knew, and I wasn't afraid. It was simply a question of will.

John Burnside

'That's it,' I called. 'You're right there.'

'Yes, but—'

'Reach right in. I'm telling you—' I raised the pole and trained it out over the water, like some huge fishing rod. It trembled and wavered and for a moment I was afraid that it wouldn't be up to the job.

'There's no nest here—' he said. He was just beginning to sound genuinely annoyed. The pole was behind him. All I had to do was swing it and push. I had practised this—but I hadn't taken into account the possibility that he might turn and see what I was doing, and I hadn't taken into account how much heavier he was than any of the objects—a sack, a tree branch—that I had practised with.

'You'd better not be mucking me about—' Malcolm Kennedy turned and saw what was happening, but it was too late. Maybe it even helped me, that he was turning, and so off-balance and distracted, when the pole swung in and hit him hard and square, almost slipping from my hands as I pulled it back and prepared to swing again, excited now, suddenly certain of victory. I saw his face—he was confused, of course, but the confusion only lasted for a moment, as he saw what I had done, and that he couldn't hold on. Then he was falling, hanging in the air for a moment before he went, like a cartoon character who has just run off the edge of a cliff—and now he seemed genuinely upset, as if he had been betrayed for no reason by a true friend and not some miserable boy he had victimized for months.

He hit the water hard. I was impressed. It was a flat, slapping noise, not a splash so much as the sound the wind makes filling a sail, or the sound I had made hitting the ground, the day he had winded me. I'd got him on my first try, and he had no idea what had hit him. He went right under, then he came up, choking, splashing about desperately, the water in his nose and mouth, his face scared. With only a fleeting sight of him to go on, I could see he really was afraid. He was frightened. He didn't know what had happened, and now he was in the pit and there was no way out. From the level he was at, there was no way he could reach up and pull himself out, all he could do was swim about, or tread water, waiting for someone else to help him. I stood for a moment, watching him surface, wanting to be sure that I had accounted for everything, that there was no way he could climb back out and come after me. Then I turned and walked far enough into the shadows that he couldn't see me. I couldn't see him either, but I had already seen enough. He was afraid. He didn't know what had hit him. That was all that mattered.

Finally he spoke. 'What the fuck!' he said. 'Hey!' I could hear him splashing around in there, trying to get to the side. Not that there was much point. He wasn't going anywhere. I stood listening, savouring the moment. Then he shouted again. 'You better get me out of here,' he said. 'Or your life won't be worth living.'

I didn't say a word. It was time to go. Leave him to stew. Let him know how it felt to be afraid. Let him know how it felt to be humiliated. I was tempted to take one last look, just to see him splashing about in all that filthy water, but I exercised self-control. I reined myself in. After all, I was there to make a point, not to gloat. Mrs Collings would have been proud of me.

All the way back to town, I was sure he would come to no real harm. He would be found, after a suitable delay; someone would hear his cries and haul him out and I would see him at school—chastened, or in vengeful mood—the following Monday. He would have had the whole weekend to think about what had happened, and maybe to plan new attacks against me, but I didn't care. For that day, at least, I felt I had done something, I felt *strong*. If it all began again, I would begin my own campaign again, and I would catch him out, too, sooner or later. I knew my own strength now. And who knows? Maybe he'd decide to get himself a different special friend.

At the same time, though, I have to confess that the thought crossed my mind, not once, but several times, that he might drown out there and, though I didn't linger over this notion, I know that it didn't bother me. I didn't care about him, and I knew there was nothing that could connect me with his apparent accident. For that next hour or two, I felt elated at having done what I wanted to do and, if I gave thought to it at all, the only thing I was certain of was that, if Malcolm Kennedy drowned, I would be free of him. Not that I ever considered this a serious possibility. He wouldn't drown, because nobody drowned in a twelve-foot-deep pit of water, a few miles from the town.

When I got to town, I went into the baker's and bought myself a little bag of doughnuts, the ones I liked. It was starting to get cooler, and the doughnuts felt warm in my hand; I ate two, then I closed the bag, so I'd have some for later. They tasted delicious. those two doughnuts. Sugared, warm, doughy, a little chewy. I felt good, too good to just go home. I decided I would walk over to Sandhaven, then come back the roundabout way, along the old railway line. The sun was starting to dip over the water, but it wasn't cold, just pleasantly cool. To be honest, I didn't think about Malcolm Kennedy. I think I kept him out of my thoughts on purpose, not to spoil the moment. Because some moments you want to last forever. Moments of freedom, moments when you know exactly who you are and that what you are doing is exactly what you were meant to be doing. ☐

GRANTA

VICTORY IN LEBANON
Wendell Steavenson

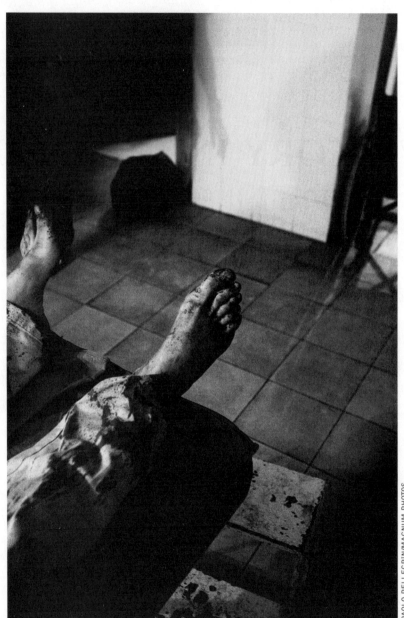

On a Wednesday morning in July, a Hezbollah paramilitary unit ambushed an Israeli patrol on the Lebanese border, killing three soldiers and kidnapping two; on Thursday morning, at dawn, Israeli jets bombed Beirut's airport. The switch flipped from peace to war, blink, Lebanon was blockaded; out of a clear blue summer sky came the bombs.

I was living in a Christian neighbourhood of Beirut near the port. I stockpiled pasta, rice, corned beef, cans of tuna, enough bottled water for a month and five cases of beer, and watched as the streets of Beirut emptied. Israel was mainly bombing infrastructure—highways, bridges, fuel reserves for a power station—in the southern suburbs, about five or six kilometres away. But in those first few days it was hard to know for sure. When the bombs woke me up at four a.m., I went downstairs and sat with my neighbours, shared a cup of coffee, three or four cigarettes. They shrugged with bravado and recalled the civil war—much worse, they said—and we watched the rubble pile up on the TV news. During the day, I went around the schools and interviewed some of the hundreds of thousands of Shi'a families displaced from the southern suburbs of Beirut and villages in the south. I watched foreigners evacuate on car ferries to Cyprus and listened to pundits speculate. On the edges of the emptied Shi'a neighbourhoods, suddenly unemployed men sat in cafes, worrying, trying to call brothers in southern villages, where the mobile signals were dead, complaining, raging against Israel and America—always uttered as one word, 'IsraelAmerica'—and cheering when Hezbollah hit a warship.

I wanted to see where the stories were coming from, so I went south with a driver and another reporter to the ancient port of Tyre. The BBC was reporting an almost constant bombardment of the surrounding hills. The route was difficult and scary. The highway bridges were bombed out; it took three and a half hours to drive through the sheer Chouf mountains, struggling through bottlenecks of refugee traffic coming the other way. South of Sidon there was no traffic at all. We got lost trying to find the crossing over the Litani river, through a limestone quarry, up a narrow dirt track through orange groves and banana plantations. The roads were deserted and cut with bomb craters. We kept having to double back to find the way. The air was still and heavy; puffs of smoke from bombing in the hills rose in slow motion.

In Tyre in the evenings the only thing to do was to sit in the old port, drink beer and watch the sunset turn pink. The fishermen, all Christian, unable to take their boats out, had taken to dynamiting fish in the shallows. At night they sat about, got drunk and railed indiscriminately at 'the Hezbollah idiots', at the Israelis and their bombs, at their own useless government and at the aid agencies who distributed canned food 'of very bad quality'. Above us a silver sliver of jet wheeled past the new moon and illumination flares hung in the darkening sky, falling slowly like Chinese lanterns in a shadow play. The stars came out and we tried to pick out the satellites. The distant hills flashed with orange explosions. The fishermen and the harbour cats and I stood in a semicircle like an audience at a sound and light show.

'Wait! Count to ten and you'll hear the blast—'

In the mornings I went to the Red Cross headquarters to ask for news. The Red Cross volunteers were jolly and young and energetic. One was a painter by trade and had decorated the offices by spattering red paint on white walls, like Jackson Pollock. It looked like a bloodbath.

One morning I heard there were injured coming into the Najem hospital, on the southern outskirts of Tyre. We drove straight there. The road out of the centre of the city went past a Lebanese army garrison, an open tract which the municipality was digging up for a temporary mass grave, and a giant crater in the road with a red car in the bottom. There was a scattering commotion in front of the hospital as I arrived; a missile had hit the road, missing a car, only moments before. The car had crashed into a barrier and the family inside, fleeing their village further south, had just managed to get out before the car burst into flames.

In the emergency room surgeons in greens shouted for calm as two men were wheeled in on gurneys—they were stripped to their underpants, their bodies black-pepper-blasted, cut and bloodied, their arms flailing. Women in black chadors ran in after them, screaming, 'Where is he! Where is he!' A baby with thin trails of blood on its neck from blown eardrums was carried in by a nurse; its face was white and frozen, in shock, uncrying. I flattened myself against a wall and took out my notebook, but there was nothing to write except half-scratched sentences. A nurse stood in the middle of it all shouting, 'Who are its parents?' An old woman in a wheelchair, abandoned in the middle of the mess, trembled and could not speak. Outside there was a bang as the engine of the burning car exploded. We all flinched.

Three civilian cars were hit that morning and families were split up between different hospitals. Upstairs at the Najem there were wounded in almost every room. In one an eight-year-old boy with a burned face swathed in lotion lay on a gurney. His mother leaned over and wailed his pain for him. There had been nine of them in the car, she said, trying to reach Tyre to get out by boat. The boy looked up through purple, swollen, gummed eyelids and asked his mother, 'Am I going to die?'

She shook her head and then cried again.

'When is Dad coming?' His father had been killed in the strike.

'Leave Dad alone now.'

I found two brothers, Ali and Abbas Shaito, sitting in a room with their cousin Hiba. A long drip of blood bisected Hiba's forehead and she was gingerly resting a bandaged hand on her lap. Her face was pale; she had a delicate beauty and green watery eyes. The brothers were sitting side by side on the edge of a bed, bloodied and bandaged, answering questions from the nurses and from me, breaking into tears, trying to find their sister. They told the nurses, 'Please look! She is fifteen. She was wearing blue.'

The Shaitos came from Tiri, a southern village set into a gully a few kilometres from the border. Most of the extended family lived in Beirut's southern Shi'a suburbs and returned to the village at weekends and in the summer. They had sheltered in a relative's house there when the war began, fifty of them together. Twelve days passed. The children wailed through the bombing, the toddlers imitating the boom-boom noises, and food began to run short. All day, all night, they could hear Israeli drones humming overhead. Hiba's father, Mohammed, was always fond of birds and he had brought a bulbul, a little songbird, with him to the house; one night, driven mad by the bombardment, it flew into a wall and died.

The Shaitos had only three cars and no one wanted to have to divide the family into who went and who stayed. Finally it was decided to send as many as they could in the three cars, and the rest would hire a minivan and driver to take them the next day. A sum of $1,000 had been agreed. In the morning, the driver arrived with his minivan and the eighteen remaining Shaitos packed in: Ali and Abbas and their sister and their mother; Hiba and her sister; her parents, their grandmother and several others. Ali and Abbas's father, Yayah, Hiba's brother Amin, and Hiba's fiancé stayed behind: they had their duties.

The driver locked the doors so that they wouldn't fly open around the bends as he drove, and set off. He drove fast through the hills of southern Lebanon, past deserted villages and petrol stations blown to ashes. There were craters in the road and sometimes the driver had to slow down and coax the van, low on its axles, across the earthen culverts. Around a bend, the road fell steeply into a valley to their right; on their left was a hill planted with an olive grove. Ahead they saw a car that had been hit only a few minutes before. It was still smoking. The driver was dead—there was just a black figure of solid unmoving shadow at the wheel—but his passenger was crawling on the ground injured. He seemed to be calling to them or reaching to them. The driver, worried, drove faster. Some of the Shaitos said they should pick him up, but he did not want to.

'No, we cannot stop,' he said. Then a missile hit the road close. The explosion swayed the van and the windows broke into tiny, nicky pebble pieces. Ali thought to himself, '*Khalass*, that's finished, we're gone now. They are going to hit us.'

Then the second missile hit. There was a silence of shock and burst eardrums. Everyone was covered in blood. Still they were quiet; no one screamed. Ali and Abbas had their clothes torn to shreds, their faces blasted with sooty debris. 'When we were hit,' Ali said, 'there was no sound, only blood splashing.' The missile had hit almost directly in the centre of the roof of the van and torn a ragged hole. Underneath the hole sat the half-headless body of Hiba's father, Mohammed, his arms resting surreally on the window. Ali jumped from the window and dragged his mother to safety. Their sister Ghadir hopped, her whole face red with blood, holding her left hand awkwardly.

It took twenty minutes, maybe a little longer, for the Red Cross to reach them. Behind the ambulances were two or three cars of journalists. As an aunt was prised carefully out of the wreckage and the rest of the survivors loaded into ambulances, a photographer knelt and took pictures of Ali's mother reaching with her hand to touch her son's face. Mother and child; almost a pietà. Her left arm was nearly severed at the bicep and she was almost unconscious with pain. She looked up at Ali and told him to take care of his brother Abbas and his sister Ghadir. Then her eyes rolled back into her head.

All this Ali and Abbas told me later, at the hospital. A nurse stopped at the door and asked if anyone knew who the parents of an eight-month-old baby were. Ali kept repeating, 'My grandmother was still breathing. She was still breathing. She was trapped inside and no one could get her out.' Hiba nodded, quiet, very still and fragile, as she told me her father was dead.

A li, Abbas and Hiba were evacuated to Beirut. I went back to the capital, too. The hospital in Beirut was the same as in Tyre: a war of corridors. A juxtaposition of clean white blandness and sobbing figures in black; of efficient nurses and X-rays and the mess of torn flesh that the bandages hid. Everywhere journalists tried to jot down particulars of scabbed faces, yellow bruised jaws, loops of IV tubes. The stories seemed all the same, the war flattened into two dimensions: large bombs and bleeding civilians. A stark, uneven propaganda. The photograph of Ali and his mother was printed on the front page of newspapers all over the world. Ali and Abbas's sister needed plastic surgery on her face; their mother had pins put in her arm.

Shaito relatives kept sombre vigil. The women were wrapped in black hijab; the men were piously courteous, touching their right hand to their heart in greeting instead of shaking my hand. For days, their lives seemed narrowed to the corridor itself. The Shi'a under bombardment retracted into outraged victimhood and leaned on sufferance for solace.

'Somehow God will revenge all of this.'

'Be patient, God will revenge. They are suffering as we are suffering. They will go back to the diaspora, in time, and they will suffer what we are suffering now.'

Hiba had moved her gold engagement ring from her bandaged right hand to her left. She introduced me to her brother, called Haidar, a policeman who guarded the Cypriot embassy. She was leaning on his shoulder for support; he was whispering to her the bereavement mantra of patience. He was barely twenty, tall, taut, lithe, with black winged eyebrows and a sense of brooding, coiled temper, cut with a wide, shy smile. He was dressed in the sharp uniform of Shi'a cool: tight jeans with architectural seams and a tailored black shirt with white stitching detail and poppers on the cuffs. Around his neck was a heavy silver chain with a sword of the martyr Ali. His hair was grease-gelled into curly, spiky quiffs and the fingernails of his pinkie fingers were grown long.

A week later Haidar met me in a cafe in deserted downtown Beirut. It was a Sunday afternoon and we could hear the heavy thuds as the southern suburbs were being bombed. A few days before, he had driven south to retrieve the body of his and Hiba's father from the minivan. The body had been there for ten days, foetid and rotting. He said his father was just a yellow inflated torso with legs; dogs must have taken the arms.

'Even if I am dead I will see this scene, even when they are putting me in my own grave.'

I could feel Haidar's distracted energy, angry and helpless. He kept calling friends in the southern suburbs to see what buildings had been hit and getting up to check the ticker-tape news scrolling across the TV screen.

'They are going to hit every building with a Hezbollah flag on it.'

I saw Haidar a couple of times in those middle weeks of the war. He was in a torment and he seemed to swing between laughing depression and bravado fear. He was not sleeping; every day there was more bombing in the southern suburbs and he would take his moped and speed down there, looking for new damage, drawn to the danger, escaping, returning. He told me, 'I feel like I am going to explode.'

Once Haidar showed me a photograph on his mobile phone. It was taken on Jerusalem Day, the Israeli national holiday on which Hezbollah organizes martial displays in front of crowds waving green and yellow flags with the party's fist and Kalashnikov logo. It was a picture of a Hezbollah paratrooper in full camouflage fatigues, black webbing and an M16 across his chest and a black balaclava over his head, abseiling down a building for show.

'This is my brother Amin,' he told my translator proudly, and then recanted—Hezbollah secrecy—telling him to say it was a neighbour instead.

But now Haidar had received a telephone call from a sheikh in Tiri with the news that Amin had been seriously wounded. Amin was older than Haidar, disciplined, pious, modest, fair-haired and well thought of. Haidar said that people were always telling him he should be more like his brother; he twitched a laugh, shrugged. He was trying, but—his father was dead, his elder brother may be dying too. I asked him how he felt about his brother. He tried to be patient in the face of God's will.

'He has chosen this road and you can't get sad about it.'

As the war continued, the suspension of normal life dissipated into a sludge of endurance. No one I met in Beirut could even be bothered to speculate any more on what the Israelis would do next, or whether Hezbollah would be blamed for the war and its toll on civilians. After a month it looked likely to escalate still further. The Israelis stepped up their assaults in the south, and Hezbollah continued to fire rockets at Haifa. But then a UN resolution was finally reached, and a ceasefire heralded for the following Monday. It seemed tenuous, too much to hope for, even unlikely; on the phone Haidar said he didn't believe it.

At eight a.m. that Monday morning in the middle of August, the hour of the ceasefire that no one yet trusted, we went back to Tyre. We drove over makeshift wobbling planks that were the only river crossing into the city. The roads were empty, the atmosphere uncertain, the route to Tibnine, in the interior south, not yet open. These were bomb-scarred villages, still littered with smoking ashy gaps of collapsed buildings and smashed petrol stations. Fields of concrete rubble were strewn across the road. We inched behind the Caterpillar diggers clearing wreckage from the final, overnight bombardment. Hezbollah men driving beat-up BMWs, bearded, serious, cagey, with walkie-talkies in their back pockets, pointed out scattered cluster bombs and told us to drive cautiously in the tracks of the diggers. I watched the diggers' claws drag broken electrical cables to the side of the road. A knot of local teenagers with sparse beards gathered, blinking in the sun of the strangely peaceful morning, and commented on their survival.

'By the Resistance we are safe!'

'At night it was hard. From eleven-thirty, you couldn't leave the house.'

'We won! It was a world war and we won!'

They smoked and thanked God, laughingly, that they still had tobacco.

In Tibnine there were cluster bomblets everywhere, little metal canisters with a projecting loop no bigger or more interesting than any other bit of debris—brick chunks, twisted metal rods, broken glass—scattered under the tyres of parked ambulances, in the dent of kerbs, rolled under bushes. You had to watch your step. No one was quite sure where the Israelis were. The next hill? Beit Yahoun, Hadatha, Tiri? At the Red Cross headquarters I found the director of operations, Mohammed Maki, tall, authoritative, originally from Tibnine, a Seyyed but secular. I had met him after two ambulances had been hit ferrying wounded from Tibnine to Tyre during the war. He had joined the Red Cross in 1982, the year of the Israeli invasion, and he said that in all the conflicts he had seen since, the hardest moments were when he had to listen to his own volunteers over the radio—injured, bleeding, running out of blood—and wait for the all-clear to pick them up. Maki didn't subscribe to the 'us and them' of the Shi'a and the Israelis. He remembered when everyone in the south had welcomed the Israelis with rice in '82, grateful that they had come to evict the Palestinian fighters. He remembered that in the early 1980s, before the Occupation turned sour, buses took Shi'a villagers across the border to Haifa for day trips. He told me, shaking his head at the righteousness of Hezbollah's violence, 'The Lebanese are a stupid nation! Muslims think Israel is the enemy. I don't know why they think like this, even though I am a Muslim myself.' Now he was coordinating dozens of ambulances sent to ferry the stranded wounded and dig out corpses.

'Israeli soldiers are still in places, we don't know where,' he said. He looked at his map, answered his phone, listened to the reports coming in over the radio. He gestured at the view across a valley. 'My house here in Tibnine,' said Maki, 'all the windows are smashed. They hit an ambulance right in front of it—' His radio crackled. 'I have to see where the Jews are—in Beit Jbail?'

One of the Red Cross volunteers who had been injured—lightly; his hand was bandaged in a splint—in the ambulance in front of Maki's house took us down to the basement garage of the adjacent unfinished block, which they were using as a temporary morgue. Four corpses tied up in thick plastic sheeting were laid out. As I stood there, shoe scuffing concrete, contemplating the repetitive dullness of rubble, an ambulance backed up and they began to unload a body on a stretcher. A Hezbollah fighter, face blown off the night before. A sandy-haired man appeared to one side. He had red eyes, blood under his fingernails and a walkie-talkie in his pocket. He said the dead man was his cousin. He had found his body at dawn.

'He was twenty-eight years old. He had three children. He was born in Hariss and he never left his village. He fought for his village and died in his village. Yesterday there was a battle from eight p.m. until the ceasefire this morning.' He recounted all this in a quiet monotone.

That first day of ceasefire was a slow waking, a reckoning. Peace seemed a half-forgotten thing. The fighters appeared by the side of the road, at rendezvous beneath a cracked minaret, on the steps of the hospitals, tired, drawn, often wounded. In the villages people began to look about themselves and take in the scale of destruction.

In the late afternoon I went back to the hospital in Tyre. A black SUV pulled up with a group of four wounded fighters dressed in khaki trousers, T-shirts, desert boots and trainers. They limped across the car park in the golden late-afternoon sun, one with his trousers rolled up and both calves bandaged, one with cotton wool stuffed into his ears. A few streets away some kids had set up giant speakers that were booming patriotic chants under Hezbollah flags, and people were handing out sweets to the returning refugees stuck in traffic. But inside the hospital there was no sense of victory, only a hobbled respite, pride and weariness. Relatives searched, met, embraced, wept or wailed at news of death or deliverance. That day more than a hundred fighters were admitted to the main hospital in Tyre; for the surgeons it was a gore of gangrene, worms and amputations. I walked to the elevator past a woman chanting a Shi'a mourning lament.

On the third floor a fighter in a wheelchair had learned that his brother was lying in a hospital bed down the corridor, also injured, with a blasted foot. He was so overcome to see him alive, he tried to walk. 'My brother is here, really? It is my brother?' He levered himself out of the wheelchair but he couldn't stand; the nurse came to help him. He made it to the edge of his brother's bed, held his brother's hands, kissed them and kissed his forehead.

'How was your situation?'

'Rahid was martyred!'

They began to talk about their battles, puffing their exploits. 'I saw twelve Israelis torn apart on the field!'

'Where I was, I tell you there were fifty bodies of Israelis!'

Outside the emergency room another fighter, slight with a lined face covered with scabs and one eye heavily bandaged, sat waiting on a stoop. A missile had blown up in his face. He asked me if I wanted to see his wounded eye and I nodded, so he pulled up the bandage. His eyeball was bright blood red; pus wept in the corner. He would need an operation, but they said he would keep his sight. When he said his village was close to Tiri, I asked him if he knew anything about Hiba and Haidar's brother Amin, but he didn't recognize the name. He told me he had been attacked with missiles six times. I tried to josh as gently as I could. 'Well, you had some help from above, I think.'

He smiled back modestly and pulled out a length of prayer beads around his neck, kissed them and looked up to God in heaven. 'Imagine one man hiding under the trees and the fighter plane is looking for him, the fighter plane that cost hundreds of millions of dollars, and it cannot find one man one hundred and seventy-five centimetres tall, sixty kilograms in weight...'

On the second day of the ceasefire I set out for Tiri to see if I could find out what had happened to Amin, Yayah and the rest of the Shaito family. I stopped at Tibnine to confer again with Mohammed Maki at the Red Cross. He told a black post-war anecdote: a man had stopped an ambulance outside a village and flashed a V sign at the Red Cross drivers. Victory! 'No,' said the man. 'Two. There are just two houses still standing in the village.'

All along the roads in the villages in the south Hezbollah had strung up yellow banners:

WE STAYED; WE WERE PATIENT

WE WON THE BATTLE

RICE: THEY WILL NOT SEE UR NEW MEDEAST

Up towards the border, the land stood still, scarred, ochre and sinuous. Along the road, stone terracing, olive groves, fields of dry gold tobacco, purple thistles, goats nuzzling in the needle shade of a few pine trees, cacti and fig trees; in the villages, concrete houses bitten with shell-holes. We drove under arches with pictures of Khomeini, past an old woman sweeping rubble into dust clouds, past wheat fields with burnt patches, craters, boulders, shallow tank embrasures, upturned wedges of road, wrecked cars. The fizz of cicadas filled the air.

'To Tiri. Okay ahead?' I asked a man on a tractor dragging the carcass of a bloated cow behind him. He waved me on towards the border frontline. Apart from a couple of fighters sitting sullen in a car with a smashed windscreen, he was the only person I saw to ask.

On the ridge above Tiri I saw the antennae of a UN base in Lebanon, and next to it a field full of collapsed and abandoned Israeli tents. The village below seemed deserted. There was a house pancaked into concrete layers, tank tracks scratched into the tarmac, the bullet holes of small-arms fire. From the opposite direction came a red car and I stopped and asked them through the window, 'Yayah Shaito? We're looking for Yayah Shaito.'

The two men in the car brightened, recognizing the name, and told us to follow them. They'd just been watching Israeli tanks withdraw over the ridge. They did not seem to mind a journalist's intrusion. Yayah was alive, they said, down in the village. 'But don't tell him about his brother Mohammed—he only knows there was an accident with the minivan and that his wife was injured. He doesn't know about his brother being killed.'

The centre of the village was a mess of rubble and smashed masonry; the windows in the mosque were broken. A cluster of men gathered around the car. They all seemed to be fighters: smiling, relieved, sad, proud. They went to find Yayah. One man came out of his basement, where he had been sheltering with two small children for more than a month. I peered inside: the ceiling was bowed from an artillery shell that had come through the floor of the room above it. Dank, dark, no bread, some canned food, no electricity for weeks—he said his seven-year-old son had recited *Ali Ali Ali Ali* to calm himself through the bombing. An old woman walked past; they said her nephew had been martyred and his body captured by the Israelis. She was tremulous and in tears; the men told her to be patient. Then Yayah came around the corner with a great black pirate beard. I told him I had news from Beirut, that his wife was fine, that his daughter was injured but recovering, and that his sons Ali and Abbas had been very brave.

He was pleased to hear this; he asked a little more about his wife's injuries and I explained what I knew. The men stood around. There were maybe fifteen or twenty of them, hollowed and tired like the other fighters I had seen; they wore silver Qu'rans on chains around their necks, their pinkie fingernails were kept long. 'Hiba?' one asked. A young man pushed forward, thin face, lank hair: it was Jamil, Hiba's fiancé. His black hair was longer than in the picture Hiba had once shown me, and flopped into his eyes. His forearm was bandaged; he had a red scratch across his nose. He said his arm was not too bad, a little burnt. A burst from an Apache helicopter had killed a friend standing next to him. The others handed me a can of pineapple juice and teased Jamil about Hiba.

'Don't talk to him about Hiba! His heart is beating so hard when he hears her name. Look, he will start crying!'

Jafar, a fighter with dirty blond hair and an easy-going air, went to get a rucksack they had found on the body of an Israeli bulldozer driver they had killed. He roared back on his dirt bike; in the tenuous calm it sounded like a tank grinding up the road. It made me nervous, which made him laugh. It was an ordinary black rucksack with red Hebrew lettering on it. Inside, a life for a few days: underwear, an empty can of Red Bull, a packet of Winston cigarettes.

'Red Bull—look, he needed energy to drive his bulldozer,' one of them said.

'Does it work, Red Bull?'

'Yes, when I went on Haj I had two cans. It really keeps you awake.'

They had the dead Israeli soldier's wallet and they showed me his army card. A young man, born in 1981, handsome, olive-skinned— he looked the same as the circle of faces peering into his personal effects. He could have been any one of them and there was a respectful quiet as they recognized this, sifting through the redundant credit cards, turning on his mobile phone—it still had some power and the display came up in Hebrew.

Jafar pulled out a picture of the dead soldier's baby son. Then he took his own wallet out with a picture of his own son, the same age with the same chestnut curls. The dead Israeli was a mirror.

'It was too bad he had children. Poor guy,' said Jafar, enmity spent.

'He was small. He was not a big man,' said one of the men.

'In a way he was just like us.'

That evening I sat on the deserted beach in Tyre with a group of doctors from the hospital. They were all against Hezbollah and laughed because all the nurses in the hospital supported Hezbollah. The picnic was a chance to let off steam. There was beer and pizza, the surf lapped against the Roman ruins, and above us Venus hung low and bright. Someone remarked that Hezbollah was capitalizing on its victory. A surgeon took umbrage: 'This is a victory? How can I believe I am victorious? I am sure Israel won this war: Every piece of infrastructure is destroyed in Lebanon. They lost one hundred and twenty-four soldiers. We lost more than one thousand two hundred, and only ten per cent of these, maybe, were soldiers, the rest civilians— we lost everything in this war. The Israelis nothing.'

In the morning one of the Shaito aunts called me from Beirut. Amin was alive! They had all feared the worst, but he was alive. He had a dislocated shoulder; a rocket had landed nearby and catapulted a stone into him. I learned that they would bury Haidar and Hiba's father and grandmother the following day in Tiri.

The funeral cortège, two ambulances and a line of dusty cars, arrived at Tiri in the beating-hot noon. The medics, wearing surgical masks against the stench, unloaded the coffins as the villagers came down the road to the cemetery. Three sisters injured in the minivan were helped down the road, white bandages peeking out from the sleeves of their black hijab robes.

Haidar threw his arms around two of his father's sisters. Then his anger rose and he scrabbled down the rocky track, lashing out at the wing mirror of a car with his fist, smashing it. His cousins and uncles tried to calm him. He kicked at the dust and rubble with his feet; he could not be held, broke free of them and stalked downwards towards the cemetery.

Haidar's widowed mother had retrieved her husband's medicine bag from the wreck of the minivan. She held up the clear plastic zip-bag and waved it. 'I have his medicine, oh! He does not need his medicine now!'

The men stood in lines and prayed by the coffins. The clutch of villagers passed around bottles of water and murmured condolence.

'We thank God. God chose them as martyrs, the noblest people on earth.'

'We are from God and we return to God.'

'Don't cry. Your tears will burn the dead. They have been chosen by God almighty.'

Women cried, one man staggered off and was sick. The dust rose.

At the grave site, holes had been clawed in the rock red earth with a mechanical digger. The coffins were manhandled into position and sealed with concrete slabs. The digger puffed black smoke like a funerary dragon. There was no ceremony, just dirt and clots of people holding each other and weeping. Hiba cried on Jamil's shoulder and he reached up his bandaged arm to tenderly pat the back of her chador's neck. She watched them lower her father into the earth and she called out, 'Be careful of his head!'

We stood in a small patch of resinous pine shade, listening to a passing Israeli drone.

'It's dangerous here. What will happen? Tomorrow is the fourth day of the ceasefire. What will happen if the Lebanese army doesn't come? It will begin again?'

An old woman rocked a baby. A burnt uncle wept tears down his piebald face. An aunt hugged me and said, 'Mohammed, now every day he is in Tiri, not just at the weekend. Now every day he is in the place he loves the best.' Amin wiped his tears on the collar of his shirt. The grave diggers rested their hands on top of their spades and then resumed shovelling. Haidar stood alone, rebuffing comfort, watching the final movements as they filled in the grave of his father.

Later, after the wake, Haidar walked me back to the car past a cache of captured Israeli supplies, oil drums and cans of chicken supreme kept near the mosque. He thanked me for coming. Then he offered me an Israeli cigarette and a terrible epigraph: 'Without this faith, all fighting would be suicide.'　　　　□

GRANTA

THE COURTHOUSE
Tahmima Anam

'Dear Milord. No. Dear Your Lordship. Dear Judge-Saab. Dear Sir. My son Sohail is seven years old. He was born on July 8, 1952. I thought he would be a girl because I never felt tired, not once. Even though my husband told me to rest, I was always running around; I even planted hydrangeas that year. The day he came I sent for the midwife and she told me to squat and push and he didn't make a sound, just looked up and told me he was going to be my Lucky Boy. He looks just like me, though I fear he has inherited his father's unruly eyebrows; someday he will have to keep a special comb in his pocket. I tried to give him books for children, like *Five Go to Smuggler's Top* and *Mystery of the Flying Express*, but he climbed into my steel almirah and found *Wuthering Heights*, the copy I rescued the day my father had to sell his first editions to the debt collector. My daughter, Maya, is dark and thin, like her father, and already she has caused me tears because of her steely will. But she sings, Your Lordship, and not childish rhymes, she has already started on the ghazals. Milord, Your Judgeship, the children are still in a state of shock at the untimely demise of their father. They need me, and their home, to ease the burden on their little hearts. Please, take pity. Take pity. Take pity.'

As she rehearsed her speech, Rehana felt the thickness of her tongue and thought, the poets are wrong, the taste of defeat is not bitter but salt. She leaned on the gate, here in front of the house, despite the sun blazing powerfully above her, unchecked, a punishment. She closed her eyes against it, against the moment, and was exactly this way, still and salty and hot, hearing nothing, not the chime of the ice-cream man, or the lazy passing of stray rickshaws, or the cries of the vegetable and fish hawkers, when Mrs Chowdhury came out of her gate at No. 12 with a packet of glucose biscuits and a glass of water. She made a wide-hipped beeline for Rehana.

'Where have you left the children?' Rehana asked, shielding her eyes with a hand.

'They're playing with Silvi. You should eat something.'

'You know I can't do that.'

'So thin,' she heard Mrs Chowdhury mutter, and she, too, expelled a tired breath at hearing the familiar phrase. Yes, she was thin. As thin as any woman could be without disappearing, she had overheard once on a visit to the gin-rummy ladies, snapping their card wrists at the Dhaka Gymkhana Club. Why should anyone be surprised? Still, she couldn't help feeling self-conscious, a little ashamed at the way people looked at her, as though they were afraid of contracting her misfortune. Her hair had grown long, and she had started wearing it loose, like a cape, covering the pointed shoulders, the jutting-out clavicles. Her eyes she could not hide; they dominated her face, great pools of black, reflecting nothing, only giving away what was within: a swell of held-in sorrow.

'Why don't you drink some water at least?'

Rehana swallowed. 'I can't break my fast in the middle of the day.'

'You should let me come to the courthouse with you.'

'It's nothing. The lawyer says judges don't just give children away.'

But in the slight pause before she said it, and in the way she held her arms so stiffly before her, and how she had pinned her sari so tightly that it had pressed flat against her forehead, and how she didn't complain of the heat or even wipe the sweat from above her lip, Rehana revealed her uncertainty; it was entirely possible the judge would force her to give up the children. She was a widow. She had no money. And here were her husband's elder brother and his pretty, film-star wife, generously offering to take them in.

Mrs Chowdhury sighed and turned back across the road. As she ambled away Rehana nervously dipped into her purse and touched the photograph that lay within. She told herself she would not take it out again; it was already worn with her looking. Sohail was in her arms, six months old, a fat, serious child. Looking straight into the camera, Rehana radiated an unchecked happiness. It was her husband's eye behind the lens, her son's weight against her chest, and joy, it seemed, was plentiful and cheap. She had not even given Sohail a black mark on the forehead to ward off the evil eye.

Before it turned the corner, Rehana heard the shiny newness of Faiz's car approaching; she heard the hiss of the radiator grille, the throb of the engine. If she concentrated, she could even hear the pleasure Faiz took in sitting at the back with his wife while their driver navigated the dusty, winding streets.

The car stopped in front of the gate. Faiz waited while the driver hurried out and opened the door for him. Then he emerged, slow-motion, first with his polished shoe, then with the soft drape of his suit, to smile tightly and greet her.

'Rehana.'

'Brother,' she replied, moving towards the front seat.

'Sit at the back,' he insisted, trying to be kind, 'with your bhabi'. And he opened the door. As she lifted her sari to step into the car, Rehana noticed she had forgotten to change out of her rubber house-slippers. She thought about asking them to wait while she went back, but decided against it; it was getting late; they would roll their eyes impatiently and consider it another symptom of her misfortune.

It was a different world inside, close and airless and full of the collective scent of Faiz and Parveen. Rehana felt a quiet longing as she breathed in the heaviness of Parveen's perfume, the rounded, buttery warmth of Faiz's pomade. She imagined herself gripping the back of the seat, her fingers pressing into the cream leather and releasing its fragrance, new and factory-bright, and saying, please, please don't take my children. I beg you. I beg you, for the sake of my dead husband—your brother, Faiz—to let me keep them. With their mother. But instead she leaned awkwardly against the seat and tried to smile at Parveen.

Sitting beside her, Rehana felt brittle and small.

As Faiz's wife, Parveen was comfortable in shape and position. A sharp face—chiselled, people had called it in her actress days—had softened and settled. She was still pale, still had that narrow nose, the bow-and-arrow lips, only now she had the self-possession of a rich man's wife, her earlier fame a mere side note. Faiz had forbidden any more films, and Parveen happily agreed, proud of her husband's jealousy. But they had no children, and when Parveen wasn't looking, Rehana saw a kind of greed etched on her prettiness.

'How are you today, Rehana? Feeling better?' Parveen asked.

Rehana wondered what answer she might give. They assumed it was a matter of resolve, like recovering from an illness. She started to reply, but changed her mind and said nothing. Fixing her gaze on the road as they drove past her neighbours' houses, the shutters closed to the force of the afternoon sun.

'This heat!' Parveen said. 'Only March and such heat!' She took out a red-and-blue polka-dot fan from her handbag and began passing it back and forth across her face in quick, restless movements.

Dhaka, the almost-city, shook beneath the wheels of the car. Made out of a colonial outpost, it was now called upon to perform the duties of a capital; it laboured under the weight of such expectation, and this gave the city its air of accident, the empty expanses of hastily covered delta swimming beneath the asphalt of new roads; large plots of land beside the signs of decay; newness and rot jostling for space.

As they left Dhanmondi Rehana noticed a hush on the streets, as though everyone had decided at once to stay indoors, or if they had to venture out, to do so sparsely, in ones and twos. Even the air seemed not to move, the giant banyan trees silent on the side of the road.

'What's happened?' Rehana heard herself say.

'Martial law, sister! Don't you know?'

Yes, of course she knew; she just hadn't cared. So this was what it looked like: a quiet day, people's sorrows hidden inside them like relics.

'Putting order to the mess we have made of ourselves.'

Parveen looked out of the window and quickened the pace of her fanning.

'I don't care what anyone says,' Faiz continued. 'Authority is what we need.'

Rehana had stopped listening; they were driving past Ramna racecourse. She couldn't see inside, but in the distance, where she knew there was a field, a pair of kites chased one another, floating and dipping through the air. Perhaps there was a breeze, she thought, and wished she could open the window.

'...I don't think Iqbal would have disagreed,' Faiz said finally. But Faiz had got his brother wrong. Unlike his friends at the club, Iqbal wasn't interested in politics. He didn't get sweaty and energetic over the threat of a divided Pakistan, or where all the jute money was being spent. He was absorbed with more variable matters: the growth of the children (measured along the garden wall), the protection of his wife (against illness, the sun, the gazes of men), the prevention of rainy days. The sidestepping of consequence.

They turned into the university compound and were met with loud banners flapping from the dormitory windows. DEATH TO THE DICTATOR! they said. DEMOCRACY: PEOPLE'S RIGHT and AYUB KHAN MUST GO! As they passed the art college they saw a crude painting of a naked peasant whose back was bent before a field of paddy; men in army uniforms pointed guns at him; one of them had a whip; he cut crudely into the flesh. An enormous red sun dominated the background.

Faiz made a strange sound between a sneeze and a laugh, as

though waiting for some provocation. 'Dogs,' he said with a grunt.

Rehana took out her photograph and stared hard at it, willing her tears to remain balanced in the crease of her eyelids, not spilling down her cheeks, not tracing the line of her nose, not falling on to her shoulder and blooming darkly on her white sari. Parveen said only one more thing during the ride: 'It's for your own good.'

A crowd had gathered at the entrance to the courthouse: men, mostly, looking ferocious, raising their fists, their spittle flying into the air as they shouted to be let in. Rehana saw reporters, a flash, and felt the crunch of shattered glass underfoot as she stepped out of the car. There were men in green uniforms beating back the crowd, the people heaving and lurching at the gate. Faiz held up his arms and towered above everyone else, making a path for Rehana and Parveen to push through. Parveen whispered, 'Are those cameras for me?' and shielded her face with spread fingers, exposing the carefully lined eyes, drawn to look like a cat, or Audrey Hepburn in *Roman Holiday*. Rehana heard a few scattered words—*dictator*, *coup*, *house arrest*—before pushing through the doors.

The halls within were quieter, but still crowded, peons and clerks and petty officials making way for the lawyers who swayed casually through the corridors. Faiz was leading the way and Rehana followed through the maze of passages and verandas. She saw a young man who looked a little like Iqbal kneeling beside a bench and assembling a sheaf of papers. He was worried; a triangle of skin gathered at his forehead as he glanced at the papers distractedly, arranging, rearranging. He dropped something with a clatter and said, 'Damnit!' under his breath, and Rehana stopped, bent to pick it up. It was an elegant, gold-tipped pen. The man thanked her, red-faced, and muttered, 'My father's.'

'What are you doing?' she found herself asking.

'He's been jailed. Our assets are frozen.' He looked around and then said, in a low voice, 'My father was an MP. Ayub's been out to get him for years.'

'Your mother?'

'She's depending on me. And I have three sisters.' The triangle deepened. 'And you? Do you mind if I ask?'

Rehana closed her eyes for a moment, wondering if she should tell him. She wanted to reach out and pinch his forearm. 'It's nothing,' she said, for the second time that day.

'Well, good luck then. It's all up to the judge.'

No, she thought, rebuking him, up to God.

They came to a door labelled, in Urdu, 'Family Court', and as they passed through, Rehana saw her lawyer waiting for her. He flashed a smile, revealing a row of pointed teeth, and waved to the seat beside him. Rehana looked to Faiz, who had put on his gown and was frowning at the scene, as though there was a distant memory that did not match. The room was shabby, the red velvet covering the benches worn to a black shine, the ceiling displaying fans stiff and woolly with dust. Even the lamps attached to the panelled walls gave off only a weak, oily light.

The judge came into the room and flopped unceremoniously into his chair. His only concession to the ritual was the curled white wig he had tossed on his head. The grey ringlets appeared tattered, his own black hair protruding from beyond the wig's reach. He pounded his gavel and got straight to the point. 'For what cause are you taking the court's time today?'

'Your Lordship, Barrister Faizul Haque. My wife and I are applying for custody of the children of my brother, Iqbal Ehsanul Haque, recently deceased, under section 146 of the Muslim Family Protection Act. We are moving to Lahore next month, Sir, and wish to take the children with us.'

'Representing Mrs Haque, Your Lordship,' the lawyer said.

'Begum Rehana Haque?' the judge said, scratching under the wig.

'Yes, Your Lordship,' Rehana replied, sounding strange to herself, as though she were someone else: a criminal, maybe, or a refugee.

'How long were you married, Mrs Haque?'

'Eight years, Your Lordship.'

'And you have two children?'

'Yes, Your Honour. Sohail and Maya. Seven and five.' She steadied herself for the speech.

'The information is all in the file, Your Lordship,' the lawyer said.

The judge riffled through some papers, cleared this throat, and began to read. 'Ah yes. Rehana Haque. Born in Calcutta to Farouq Ali,' he said. 'Lost his fortunes before Partition. Family left Calcutta, went to Karachi. Except you, Mrs Haque. You came to Dhaka to marry. Your father died shortly thereafter. Your three sisters live in Karachi. No brothers. Is that right?'

'Yes, Your Lordship.'

The judge's face remained impassive. 'You live in Dhanmondi, Road 5?'

'Yes.'

'Your own house, Begum?'

Why wasn't he asking her anything about the children? 'Yes.'

'Your husband owned Triple S Insurance Limited. What is the state of the business?' He turned to the lawyer.

'Finished, Your Lordship. Without Iqbal-saab, the business could no longer survive. But Mrs Haque will be getting an allowance.'

'How much?'

'Fifteen rupees a month, sir.' If this seemed a small sum to the judge, he did not say.

The judge turned to Faiz. 'And what is your prayer, Mr Haque?'

Faiz cleared this throat. 'Your Lordship, these are difficult times,' he began solemnly. 'What would we be without the sanctity of the family? My brother and I were very close. Our parents, peace-be-upon-them, passed away many years ago. I never imagined Iqbal would pass before I did.' He paused for an expansive sigh. 'I helped him start the company. Built it from nothing.'

'Milord, this matter is not relevant to the case.'

Outside Rehana could hear the muezzin call from the courthouse mosque. Her thoughts drifted as the afternoon pressed on. She tried not to think of Mrs Chowdhury's glucose biscuits.

The lawyer was standing up and raising his finger in protest as Faiz was finishing a sentence: '...doubts about her mental state.'

'Your Lordship,' said the lawyer, 'this allegation is completely baseless.'

'Let me hear it,' the judge interrupted. 'You will have your chance.' A slow yawn travelled through his face.

'It was a terrible tragedy,' Faiz continued, smiling indulgently, 'but I am not sure she has handled it well. After all, she is very young.'

'Your Lordship!' the lawyer shouted.

Faiz looked at Parveen with a pained expression, his hands pitched in a gesture of surrender. Parveen glanced back at her husband and nodded serenely. 'Your Lordship, it is with great regret that I say this. But Mrs Haque has conducted herself in a most inappropriate manner.'

'Please continue, Sir.'

'Rehana—Mrs Haque—has been unable to return to normal after my brother's death. She refuses to eat. She neglects the children. Sometimes they go to school without their uniforms.'

Rehana saw the judge take out a pen and begin making notes. 'Your Lordship,' she said, 'I can explain.'

'Yes please, Madam,' he replied slowly, displaying an exaggerated patience.

Should she tell him about the children now? 'My husband died in Ramzaan. I was fasting then.'

The judge did not seem to understand. His eyebrows were still lifted in query.

'He died on a Friday,' she went on, 'and it was Ramzaan. And I am still fasting.' She saw the judge regarding her now, and noticing the narrowness of her wrists, the tendons of her neck. She saw him running through the possibilities: would she be an angry widow? A sad, weeping widow? A chest-beater? Ah yes, she heard him thinking. Starving Widow. But what to do? Should she be pitied? Berated? Taught a lesson? Rehana could see the judge was not yet sure. She tucked her feet under the sari, hoping he would not notice the rubber slippers.

'You're fasting.'

'Yes.'

'As though it were still Ramzaan.'

'Yes.'

'Every day? Sunrise till sunset?'

'Yes, Milord.'

'And the children?'

'The children are fine.'

'Ask her what they eat, Milord,' Faiz said.

She suddenly couldn't remember. She tried to conjure up an image of the children at the table, munching on their favourite snacks. Then it came to her—yes, of course. 'Mrs Chowdhury. They have lunch with Mrs Chowdhury and her daughter.'

'Who is Mrs Chowdhury?'

'A neighbour, Milord,' Faiz interjected. 'No relation.' When the judge stayed silent, Faiz continued. 'Milord, she fasts every day. She doesn't eat, doesn't drink. Sun-up to sundown. And then she has iftar, as if it were still Ramzaan—all the iftar foods—dates, fried eggplant, jalebis, everything. Is this normal, Milord? And those poor children.' Faiz looked earnest, almost desperate. 'One day I went over and they were wearing their party clothes.'

'What do you mean?'

'They were dressed up!'

'Where were they going?'

'Nowhere, Your Honour. The poor lady goes nowhere.'

'They were doing a scene, Milord.' How could she explain the fatherless mystery of her children? 'I just wanted to cheer them up.'

'A scene? What scene?'

'*The Importance of Being Earnest*, sir.'

'This is nonsense,' Faiz said. 'We are wasting the court's time.'

The judge's eyes were far away. 'Yes, it's true, we are in a hurry.' And then he said, a little regretfully, 'Mrs Haque, do you really think you can take care of these children by yourself? Do you have the resources? Have you thought about what your husband might have wanted?'

At the mention of Iqbal, the events of the last three months came back in a flood. She could see him now, wrapped in his burial shroud, the cotton stuffed into his nostrils, his dark lids, his shadowy mouth. And there were Maya and Sohail standing above him and saying nothing, staring at the picture of the dead man, their noses full of attar and incense burned to hide the smell, and outside the sweets in cardboard boxes, and a white curtain pinned across the lawn to separate the mourning women and the mourning men.

'I don't know,' Rehana heard herself saying, 'I don't know what he would have wanted. He would want them to be safe, I suppose. Yes, he would want them to be safe.'

'It's not safe here,' Faiz said. 'That is why my wife and I are moving to Lahore.'

'You are willing to take care of these children?'

'I will love them as my own, Your Lordship.'

'Mrs Haque, perhaps this will give you a chance to recover.'

She hadn't taken the children anywhere. She had been reluctant to admit their father was really dead. She had refused to explain janat and the afterlife to them. And there was that time Maya had found her sprawled underneath the garden tap. She nodded to the judge.

The judge nodded back.

Immediately, she changed her mind. 'Oh no, you can't do it!'

'Please, Mrs Haque, compose yourself.'

Compose. She was a hysterical widow.

'You will take these children to Lahore?' the judge asked Faiz.

'Yes, your Lordship. There are excellent schools in Karachi. And none of this revolution business.'

Lahore was so far away. It was on the other side of a thousand miles of India. What a map they have drawn us, Rehana thought, and if I had known it would put a continent between me and my children I would have killed that map-maker myself. My son is seven years old. Seven years old. He was born on July 8, 1952. If only they had let her begin with that.

But it was too late. She looked to the right, past the lawyer and into the corridor, where the painted courthouse pillars gleamed in the afternoon sun, and to her left, where a magpie had paused on the high branch of a banyan tree. One for sorrow, Rehana said to herself. Two for joy. The judge was announcing his verdict; she tried not to hear it. If she didn't hear the words, perhaps what was to follow would not follow. The judge's gavel would not be pounded; he would not rise as though his business was finished; a flat, unpleasant smile would not make its way to Faiz's mouth; Parveen's heels would not fall satisfyingly on to the marble floor, and she would not crumple, passing the lawyer's outstretched hand, avoiding the bench that might have broken her fall. Her sari would not have ballooned around her knees. And yet, the moment did pass, the judge did his duty, Faiz and Parveen theirs, and Rehana fell, as she might, at the knowledge that she had given her children away.

The lawyer made a final attempt to change the judge's mind. 'Your Lordship,' he cried out, 'please do not make a hasty decision!'

From the ground where she lay Rehana heard the judge exhale a long, irritated breath. She heard it in snatches: 'This court's time has already been wasted...martial law...country...chaos... And then: 'That is all. Dismissed.'

Outside the courthouse Rehana bought two kites, one red and one blue, from Khan Brothers Variety Store and Confectioners. The kites were made of thin, translucent parchment paper, and were held together by slender bamboo reeds crossed in the middle and tied with a length of jute. Rehana tucked the packets under her arm and hailed a rickshaw. As she was climbing in she saw the lawyer running towards her. His belly stayed rigid as the rest of him wobbled.

'Mrs Haque, I am very sorry.' He sounded sincere.

Rehana couldn't bring herself to say it was all right.

'You must find some money. That is the only way. Find some money and then we will try again. These bastards don't move without a little grease.'

Money. Rehana stepped into the rickshaw and lifted the hood over her head. 'Dhanmondi,' she said. 'Road No. 5.'

When she got home the children were sitting together on the sofa with their knees lined up. Maya's feet hovered above the floor. Sohail was looking down at his palms and counting the very small lines. He saw Rehana and smiled but did not rise from his chair, or cry out, as Maya did, 'Ammoo! Why were you so long?'

Rehana had decided it would not be wise to cry in front of the children, so she had done her crying in the rickshaw, in sobs that caused her to hold on to the narrow frame of the seat and open her mouth in a loud, wailing O. The rickshaw puller had turned around and asked, as if he was genuinely concerned, whether she would like to stop for a glass of water. Rehana had never tasted roadside water. She refused him mutely, wondering if he had children, a thought that made her lean her head against the side of the rickshaw hood and knock, repeatedly, in time to the bumps on the road. Now, confronted with the sight of them, she fought the pinch in her jaw and the acrid taste that had flooded her mouth. She fought the fierce stinging of her eyes, the closing of her throat. She fought all of these as she handed them the wrapped-up, triangular packets.

'Thank you Ammoo-jaan,' Maya said, ripping into hers. Sohail did not open his. He rested it on his lap and stroked the brown wrapping. Then he bit down on his lip and stared at his mother.

'You are going to live with Faiz chacha,' Rehana said evenly. 'In Lahore.'

'Lahori!' Maya said, laughing.

The Courthouse

'I'm so sorry,' Rehana said to her son.
'When will we come back?'
'Soon, I promise.' Pray to God, she wanted to say, but couldn't.
'They are coming for you tomorrow morning.'
'But I don't want to.'
Rehana bit down on her tongue. 'You have to go,' she said. 'Go and be brave. You can fly your kite, beta, and I will see it, all the way from Karachi. It's a very special kite. You have to be very good. Very good and very brave. Only the bravest children get windy days. And one day it will be so windy you will fly all the way back to me. You don't believe me? Wait and see.'

In the morning the children were gone. Rehana had packed their things in a hurry, crying into the comb, the ragged copy of *Treasure Island*, forgetting to fold, jamming shoes into the corners of the trunk. Sandwiched between their clothes was a photograph of Iqbal in his three-piece suit, one thumb hooked into his waistband, another on the dial of his pocketwatch. She packed a copy of the Holy Book, then took it out. She had tried to write them a letter, but she had no words. Finally she had settled for a few mooris and a bar of chocolate.

Afterwards, when the door was shut behind them, Rehana turned to find their little things strewn over the bedroom, the corridors. A sock, a sliver of ribbon. A page from Sohail's notebook. The stray things rattled around the bungalow like a cough.

They still called it the bungalow, because it was a modest house on a vast, empty plot—a one-storey building with just two bedrooms, a drawing room, a kitchen, a wrap-around veranda. The bedrooms faced the garden and the empty land beyond; the living room and kitchen faced the street. There were plans for a grander house at the back of the property. The bungalow would be for visitors, perhaps an office. But Iqbal hadn't stayed to build the big house.

It was Iqbal's idea to buy the plot in Dhanmondi. Less than a year after they were married, he had insisted they move out of their flat on Aga Masih Lane in the old part of town. Rehana was reluctant to go; she loved the narrow streets, the smell of the Buriganga river, the shuttered buildings built by the first pioneers into the city: the river-boat owners, the traders, the Bible-wielding Jesuits. It had a sense of its own history. Dhanmondi, on the other hand, was a new residential area, just a few dirt roads carved out from the paddy. It's the future, Iqbal had said. Soon this will be the best neighbourhood in Dhaka.

And so it was. Sprawling, flat-roofed buildings set back from the road, speaking of prosperity and new money.

Rehana looked out at her tract of empty land. She had created a border with rose bushes and red hibiscus and a pair of banana trees. Inside the border was the bungalow, the small vegetable patch, and the sagging mango tree that had come with the plot. Beyond it the land was wild, the earth soft and yielding, the kind of earth that swallowed sandals and sprouted thick tufts of moss even on the coldest days.

Rehana unlatched the veranda gate and stepped into the garden. She took off her sandals and felt the grass prickling her feet, and then, a few seconds later, the cool embrace of silt between her toes. She made her way to the back of the garden, and found the small garden tap she'd used to water her roses—pink—all through the dry season. Their tired blooms surrounded her, staring as she knelt in front of the tap and pressed her forehead against it. The metal felt cool and indifferent; the water, once she twisted the knob, inviting her to squat underneath the stream, which she did, bending her neck to make it fit. She had been here before; she knew what to do.

She sat under the tap until she was fully soaked. She was not sure if she was cold. She closed her eyes and felt the poisonous sting behind them. Then she lay down beneath the tap and fell asleep.

She dreamed of her wedding night. They had lain side by side, she frozen in her brocade sari, her eyes shut, waiting for her husband to do his business. But he hadn't touched her. Once, she thought she felt his little finger brush against her elbow, but she wasn't sure if it was him or just the blanket shifting in the tense November air.

The next morning, Rehana had woken up feeling stiff and uncomfortable. The sari had scratched her knees and bunched uncomfortably around her shoulders. She found a bathroom and tugged on the taps. She pried off her make-up, rubbed the kajol out of her eyes, twisted out of the sari. She put on the starched cotton she'd been given to wear, raising it off the wet floor, avoiding the drip-drip of her long hair, and then she opened the door to greet her husband, wondering what soothing, palliative words she might offer to avert his displeasure. The door swung open, and there, on the outside lip of the doorway, were her slippers.

Who had put them there?

There was no servant. Aside from Faiz, Iqbal had no family, no fussing grandmothers, no giggling nieces. Rehana had asked her father to find her a man with few relations. A man whose fortunes had nowhere to go. And she wanted to live in Dhaka, far from the memories of their lost Calcutta, further still from the barren sprawl of Karachi, where her sisters had gone to marry.

It could only have been him. A man who brought his wife's slippers to the bathroom door. What sort of a man was this?

Rehana's devotion was born at that very moment. Not devotion of the ordinary kind; the devotion of a woman whose husband is concerned with the coldness of her feet. And that is what she dreamed of. The slippers. The possible kindness of men.

Parveen took Sohail and Maya to Karachi a few days later on the brand-new Pakistan International Airlines flight 010. Rehana watched the plane leave from an airport window made foggy by hair oil and goodbye fingerprints. She waved a small wave, wondering when the world would stop ending. Maya and Sohail, a blue kite and a red kite tucked under their arms, fastened their seat belts and sailed gracefully into the sky, crossing the flooded delta below.

The next day Parveen called to say they had arrived safely, but Rehana could hear very little aside from the crackle of the long-distance line, and the cultivated, genteel laugh that conveyed both confidence and an awkward regret.

In the days that followed, people came to see her. Iqbal's business acquaintances; old men claiming to be friends of her father; distant relatives with wagging, so-sorry tongues; the gin-rummy ladies; even the lawyer. Grief tourists, Rehana thought, and pretended not to hear them scratching at the door. All but Mrs Chowdhury, who came dragging a sad, tearful daughter. She held Rehana in the rolling fat of her arms and scolded her daughter for sulking.

'Silvi, it's not the end of the world. They'll be back.' And then she turned to Rehana. 'At least you had a few good years. My bastard husband left me when I couldn't give him a son. Took one look at this one and I never saw him again.'

Rehana sat silently and stared into the garden. Mrs Chowdhury finally said, 'We should let the poor girl rest.'

Silvi idled behind the kitchen door. 'Nine years old!' Mrs Chowdhury cried out. 'Too old to sulk, too young to be heartbroken. What, you think no boy will ever ask to marry you again?'

'Let her stay,' Rehana said. 'We can eat together.' She tried to imagine what she might feed the child. She hadn't been shopping. There was just a weak, watery dhal and some bitter gourd.

Silvi shook her head and took a crumpled envelope out of her pocket.

To: Sohail (Earnest) Haque

Karachi, West Pakistan (the Other Side of India)

'Can you send it?'

Rehana looked at the grey, sickly child. 'Of course.'

Silvi did not seem satisfied. Rehana thought the child might ask, 'How could you let them go?' But instead she said, 'You didn't let me play Aunt Augusta.'

'Aunt Augusta was a cranky old lady,' Rehana explained. 'You were much better suited to play Gwendolen.'

'Aunt Augusta has the best lines. Anyway, I'm oldest.'

'Next time, Silvi, okay?'

'If they ever come back. Okay.'

She left. Rehana didn't see her to the door.

R ehana watched the days go by. She began letters to Sohail and Maya:

The mangoes will be perfect this year. It has been hot and raining at all the right times. I can already smell the tree.

She threw that one away. She also threw away the one that began:

My dearest children, how I miss you.

She wrote cheerful, newsy letters. The children should not be confused. They should know these important facts:

She was going to get them back soon.

The world was still a generally friendly place.

Silvi had not forgotten them.

The neighbourhood was exactly as it had always been.

Her memories of the children were scrambled and vague. The more she clutched at them the more distant they became. She tried to stick to facts: Maya's favourite colour is blue, Sohail's is red. Sohail has a small scar on his chin; just below the ridge. She had teased him and said, this is a scar only your wife will see, because she will stand just beneath you and look up, and he had said, very seriously, what if she is a very tall girl?

Her son had a sense of humour. No, he was completely unfunny. He barely ever smiled. Which was it?

She took comfort in telling them apart. She remembered which was the loud, demanding child, which the quiet, watchful one. The one who sang to birds to see if they would sing back. The one whose fingernails she had to check, because she liked the taste of mud. The one who caught chills, whether the day was cold or fiercely hot; the one who sucked red juice from the tiny flowers of the exora bush; the one who spoke, the one who wouldn't; the one who loved Clark Gable; the one who loved Dilip Kumar, and stray dogs, and crows that landed on the gate with sharp, clicking talons, and milk-rice, and ice cream.

And she couldn't get out of her mind all the times Iqbal had fretted over them, making them wear sweaters when it wasn't even cold, having the doctor visit every month to put his ear to their little chests; holding hands on busy roads and empty roads; just in case, just in case, just in case. And there was that train journey a year ago, that they almost didn't take.

It was Maya's fourth birthday, and Iqbal's new Vauxhall had just arrived from England. It was on a special consignment of fifty cars brought to Dhaka from the Vauxhall factory in London, in 1957. Iqbal had seen an advertisement that told him about the smart new car with the restyled radiator and the winding handles. There was a photograph. He fell in love with the car: the smooth curves, the side-view mirrors that jutted out of the frame. He imagined driving it into their garage, a big ribbon tied around the top, the horn blaring. But when it arrived, Iqbal was too nervous to drive the car and decided to leave it in the hands of a driver he hired for the purpose, an ex-employee of the British consul-general who had driven His Excellency's Rolls-Royce and was an expert behind the wheel. His name was Kamal. It was Kamal who was driving the Vauxhall the day Maya waved to her father from the window of the Tejgaon–Phulbaria rail carriage.

As a special birthday treat for Maya, they had decided to take a train ride between Phulbaria railway station and a new station on the fringes of the city. The new tracks had just been opened and it was now a short trip to the city's heart; from the brightly painted station built by a hopeful government to the crumbling colonial building that housed the old carriages of the Raj. It was to be their very first train ride.

On the appointed day, Rehana made kabab rolls and Iqbal counted clouds, hoping to declare an incoming storm and cancel the whole affair. But there was only a cool October breeze and a scattering of lacy, translucent threads in the sky. Kamal started the car and opened the doors for them. Iqbal instructed everyone to sit in the back. Maya entered first, in her birthday dress, which Rehana had sewn of pale blue satin. There was a netted petticoat, which made the dress puff out at an unlikely angle. Blue ribbons were fastened to her hair, and she had managed to convince Rehana to dab her mouth with the lightest frost of pink lipstick; this she attempted to safeguard by keeping her lips held in a stiff pout. Rehana settled into the car, balancing the food on her lap, and motioned for Iqbal and Sohail to hurry up. But they were having some sort of argument outside.

'But Abboo, there's no space at the back.'

'You can't sit in front, it's too dangerous.'

'Oof, Abboo, I'm not a baby any more!' Sohail stomped a foot on the ground.

'Accidents can happen, doesn't matter if you are big boy or small. Accident doesn't discriminate!'

Rehana rolled down the window. 'Sohail, do as your abboo says.'

In the end Sohail piled sullenly into the car, with Iqbal following. It was tight, with all four of them in the back. Maya's dress swelled out in front of her like a small blue high tide. The netting was starting to itch, though she kept stoically still, lest she collapse the puff or wrinkle her ironed ribbons. Iqbal's white sharkskin suit was getting crumpled. Really, Rehana thought, he should have just let the poor boy sit in front with the driver. It was so hot. She rolled the window down defiantly, and motioned for Sohail to do the same on his side, not caring if they inhaled the street's dust. Maya's ribbons lapped gently in the breeze.

By the time they had reached Tejgaon, Iqbal had begun to worry about the journey again. If they were stuck on the train, how would anyone know? What if Kamal was late? He mentally calculated the odds of this happening. As Kamal drove them up to the station, he had an idea.

'Rehana, you go with the children. I have decided to stay.'

'What's that?'

'I will stay in the car with Kamal. We'll drive beside the train. That way, if anything happens, you can just leave the train and ride in the car.' Ingenious!

So that is what they did. She remembered it clearly: the man in the car, his family on the train, the train carriage on the new rail line and the new foreign car on the adjacent road, the taste of kabab rolls and lemonade lingering lazily on their tongues, and her husband, beaming to himself, satisfied at last that no harm would come to his family, because he, Iqbal, had made absolutely sure.

It was a profound arrogance, she now realized, for him to think he could save them from anything. She thought this, as outside, the mango tree pressed its fragrance into summer and, beside it, the dust-licked Vauxhall sank into the driveway. □

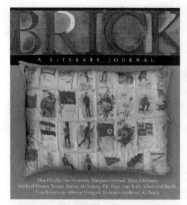
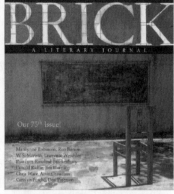

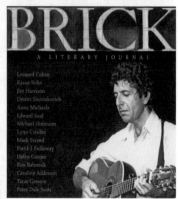

GRANTA

OPERATION GOMORRAH
Marione Ingram

Hamburg, 1945

I remember that the summer in Hamburg in 1943 was unusually dry and hot. Three of us now lived in the fifth-floor apartment on Hasselbrook Strasse: my mother, my baby sister, Renate, and me. I was eight years old and a respectful, obedient child. But one day in late July my mother asked me to do something and I disobeyed her, and I shall be forever glad that I did. She asked me to take my baby sister to my cousin Inge's apartment in another part of the city and wait for her there. We set off. I was thrilled to be outdoors, unsupervised, in charge. A cooling salt breeze from the North Sea blew through the streets and seemed to calm Renate as I pushed her along inside a grey wicker carriage with spoked wheels and a handle as high as my chin. But after a while I turned back and then began to hurry. Something wasn't right with my mother. She had cried for most of the night and hadn't told me why.

When I think of myself then, hurrying home with the pram, I also think of all the things that were unknown to me. German officials who had placed our names on deportation lists; Royal Air Force officers studying aerial photographs of our city; bombers revving on runways in the flat fields of eastern England. All of them were about to impinge on my life.

I opened the door to our apartment that afternoon and found Mother slumped on the floor in front of the kitchen stove, and for a moment I just stood there, listening to the gas jets hiss like angry geese. Because she had a six-pointed yellow star on her dress, there was no one I could call upon for help. It hadn't always been that way, but this was the summer of 1943 and those who might have helped in the past had long since been silenced.

Trying not to inhale too much gas, I pulled Mother away from the stove, tugging first one limp arm and then the other. I managed to get her head and a shoulder into the dining room, but there her clothes bunched and clung to the carpet, making further progress slow and difficult. So I took down the blackout drape that covered the dining-room window, swung back the glass pane and welcomed the air into the room and into my lungs. Mother was lying partly on one side but mainly on her back, with her eyes shut and her lips slightly parted. She was very pale and completely limp, but she seemed to be breathing.

I was sitting on the floor with her head in my lap, trying to think what to do, when coming from the bottom of the stairwell where I'd left the pram I could hear the faint sounds of my baby sister's whimpering. I slipped out from under my mother's head and ran down to fetch Renate, and then laid her beside our mother on the floor in the hope that her hunger cries would wake her. They didn't. I put a pillow under my mother's head and began to look around for something that Renate and I could eat. I found a few potatoes and filled a pot with water. Then I scratched a match and tried to light the stove, which caused a frightening flash and a loud pop and the smell of singed hair. I tried again and again, until at the third or fourth attempt the gas ring produced a steady flame. And then I cooked and mashed the potatoes and fed and changed Renate and put her on the bed where all three of us slept together when Father was away.

A year earlier there had been four of us, but Father had managed to place my middle sister, Helga, with a family that lived on a farm on the outskirts of Hamburg. With her light blonde hair, green eyes and pale skin, she was easily accepted as one more city kid farmed out among relatives to escape the bombing raids. Father wasn't Jewish. He was serving with the Luftwaffe in Belgium, not as a combat pilot but as a member of Reichsminister Goering's procurement command, which kept Germans relatively well fed at the expense of the occupied peoples. He'd been recruited by a group of Storm Troopers who had beaten him almost to death—permanently injuring his kidneys—and given him the choice of joining up or dying together with his Jewish wife and children. Father's work enabled him to supply us with enough food to survive after our ration cards were cancelled. He was also, though I didn't fully understand this then, an effective member of the Resistance—like his brother, my uncle Eugene Oestreicher, who was serving in occupied France when he chose to kill himself rather than be interrogated and tortured by an SS unit known as the 'Ascension Commandos'. On his last visit home, my father told us that his room in his Brussels pension had been searched by the Gestapo. My mother believed that Eugene's death drew suspicion on us all and that the Gestapo (to whom she had to report every week) took more than a usual interest in us as Jews.

That night I transferred Renate from the bed to the floor, put her on two pillows beside Mother, covered them with a cotton sheet and lay down next to them. There were no air raids to disturb us, though I woke up often to see if she was still unconscious. At last, in the morning, she opened her eyes and hugged and kissed Renate with tears pouring down her face.

Soon after, my cousin Inge arrived. She was the daughter of Father's half-brother and her parents ran a grocery store. They also had a Jewish woman living in their apartment, which took courage and conviction.

She was breathing hard after her climb up the five floors to our apartment. 'I was so worried about you,' she said, 'but I couldn't come earlier. Our lodger got a deportation order yesterday. She tried to take her own life while we were out at the store.'

I looked at Mother and I understood. She dried her eyes and explained that she, too, had received a deportation order: in five days we were supposed to report to Moorweide Park, the place from which all our Jewish aunts, uncles, grandparents and cousins had been taken, along with almost all of the other Jews in Hamburg. Mother told Inge that, in a desperate bid to save her children, she had asked me to take Renate to Inge's home and then tried to take her own life, hoping the authorities would not go further after finding her dead. Inge didn't say anything but simply leaned forward and took Mother's hands. Still joined, the two women sat down and searched each other's eyes and then began to talk while I made tea. The authorities had disconnected our telephone. Inge promised that she would let Father know about the deportation order as soon as possible. When she left, she took Renate with her.

That night it was unnaturally hot even for the last week of July, and breathlessly still despite the distant flashes of dry lightning. Mother and I went to bed soon after sunset. Although I was tired and glad to be in the same bed as her, I couldn't sleep because of the heat and because Mother soon began writhing and gasping and occasionally crying out in her sleep. I didn't know whether this was because of all the gas she had inhaled or because she was so upset by our deportation order. Both thoughts distressed me and I was still wide awake less than an hour later when the air-raid sirens began to wail again.

An explosion shook the building seconds later. Walls, ceilings and windows shattered and showered us with plaster and glass. Lamps and picture frames were hurled around the room. A second blast sent gale-force winds gusting through the apartment, crashing the front door to the floor, stripping mouldings, sills and sashes, overturning bookcases and tables. Then a sheet of flame flashed outside our window as a third explosion seemed to detonate inside my skull. The shock wave sent our bed skittering across the room until it tipped and spilled us on to the floor.

I was stunned. I couldn't catch my breath and I desperately had to pee, but I was too worried about Mother to stay on the floor for long. The air was thick with plaster dust and the floor slippery with broken glass. As I urinated on a crumpled heap of rug, managing somehow to remain upright and keep my panties dry, I thought I could see Mother doing the same in another corner. I tried to call out to her but we were entirely surrounded by screaming bombs and explosions. Through a large hole that had been a window I watched as the balconies of the building next door were sprayed with shards of white phosphorus, some landing on table tops, where they glowed and smouldered like strange food from outer space. Every geranium on every balcony was clearly visible in the glare of the flames. As I searched for my shoes, an incendiary bomb thudded through the roof of our building. I found one shoe and Mother the other. Unable to speak, we embraced and felt one another all over. Finding that nothing seemed to be broken or missing, we cautiously picked our way down the darkened, debris-cluttered stairway towards the courtyard at the bottom.

Draping blankets over our heads like huge shawls, we ran to the large metal door that led to the basement shelter. Mother took the nozzle of a fire extinguisher and banged on the door until it opened. A man's head in a large steel helmet poked out: it was our neighbour Block Warden Wiederman. 'What are you doing here?' he demanded.

An ear-splitting explosion answered and he slammed the door. Mother banged some more and Herr Wiederman's head reappeared. We wedged our way inside.

'You have to let us stay!' Mother shouted. 'We've been bombed out! It's certain death outside!'

Several of the people lying or sitting on bunks in the shelter got up and came over to the door. One, a rumpled, whiskered walrus of a man, held a lantern near Mother's face.

'It's the Jews!' a woman shouted. 'The Jews! The damned Jews!'

The voice was neither young nor old and there was no quality of mercy in it. In fact it seemed that the woman had progressed from surprise to indignation to outrage as she repeated herself. Explosions smothered whatever else she said and I desperately hoped others would be more compassionate; the explosions, although horrific, were much less frightening inside the bunker. But the next voice to rise above the din was Frau Wiederman's. She yelled at her husband that he had to put us out because he was in charge and it was his duty to enforce the rules against sheltering Jews.

'You'll be held responsible!' she yelled. 'Think of your family.'

'Think of us, Daddy!' It was their daughter Monika, my former playmate. She was holding her favourite doll, holding it tight and turning slightly away as if she feared I might try to snatch it from her. 'Think of us!'

The man with the lantern spoke up, his voice and breath thick with schnapps: 'Listen to your family! Put the Jews out!'

'They're going to be deported in two days,' Herr Wiederman said. 'I've seen the order myself.'

'All the more reason to boot them out,' the walrus man said.

Herr Wiederman turned to tell us to leave, but Mother interrupted, pleading with him and with the others to allow me, at least, to stay, an idea that was very upsetting to me but seemed to find some support from others in the shelter. To my relief, louder voices shouted down the soft-hearted.

'The Bolshevik Jews are behind this!' a hoarse voice growled. 'They sold us out. They told the English where to bomb.'

I found the idea exciting, but Mother said it was ridiculous.

'My husband is in the Luftwaffe,' Mother shouted. 'He's on his way here now. You will answer to him if you put us out!'

The response was angry insistence on our immediate expulsion. Frau Wiederman gave her husband a shove and he pushed open the door. Instead of going out, Mother stepped deeper inside the shelter.

'You will answer...' she shouted, and the room became silent. She didn't say anything more, but stood for several seconds looking into their faces, her eyes glistening in the lantern light. She looked hurt and angry, but cleansed of fear, almost triumphant. Instead, many of the faces in the gloom began to look fearfully at us, apparently sensing that they had damned themselves by refusing to share their private donjon. When another explosion shook the building, Mother bent with a calm, protective look and adjusted my blanket so that it covered my head. Herr Wiederman grabbed her arm to force her towards the door, but she wrenched free. Then she picked me up and walked into the street as the door slammed behind us.

A false dawn lit the south-eastern sky, rouging Mother's cheeks and painting the walls of buildings on our side of the street a lurid red. Through the openings of blasted windows we could see orange and yellow flames dancing beside pianos, making bonfires of bookcases, curling around bedposts. A torrent of hot wind coursed down Hasselbrook Strasse, bending trees almost double, stripping off branches and leaves and tugging at our blankets. Although anti-aircraft guns banged away and searchlights still probed the sky, the bombing seemed to have diminished. Along the street a gusher of water rose more than three feet above the pavement. Everything was unreal. We went back through the arched entrance to our courtyard and saw pink tulips of flame sprouting along the roofline not far from our apartment.

There were firemen in the street, which was encouraging because normally they didn't come out of their shelters while a raid was in progress. The firemen had unravelled a hose but it was flat. Although some water pressure had been restored after the raids on Sunday and Monday, the mains had been hit during the first waves of tonight's raid, creating gushers like the one we had just seen.

Some firemen across the street were working with crowbars to open the metal door of a cellar shelter, while a fireman at the top of a long ladder chopped a hole in the roof of the building next door. Although we were afraid to approach for fear of being reported, I went close enough to hear one fireman yell to another that smoke from the building next door had entered the shelter through an exit tunnel. I thought how horrible it must be for those suffocating inside the shelter and was glad for a moment to be in the street. But even as the firemen succeeded in opening the shelter door and began bringing people outside, the terrifying shrieks of falling bombs, followed by thundering explosions, announced a new wave of Lancasters or Halifaxes. Both my eardrums seemed to burst at once as a large bomb landed much too close and collapsed the wall of the building next to the shelter. We watched and moaned, 'No! No! No!' as the fireman who had chopped a hole in the roof fell with his ladder into the flames.

More bombs struck in quick succession. Most of the firemen abandoned the smoke victims and began to run for their own bunker. Two who didn't run were ripped by shrapnel and flying debris from another explosion. One fell on his face on top of a smoke victim and the other sat down on the sidewalk, holding his groin and screaming. Two firemen returned to retrieve their screaming comrade and carry him in the direction of their bunker. Many of the smoke victims were lying where they had been placed on the grassy strip beside the street, but some were staggering about, coughing and blinded, clutching at trees or lampposts for support. We lay in the gutter and watched as two or three from the shelter ran after the firemen. Following another nearby explosion we got up and chased after them, hoping that the firemen might allow us into their bunker. We ran down a narrow side street between high walls of flame until we came to a large commercial avenue. The firemen's bunker was on the other side, about fifty yards away, but the wind blowing down the avenue was filled with flying brands and was so strong that I could hardly stand in it. I lost my footing and would have gone tumbling into the flames, but Mother held on to my hand and hauled me to her side. We ducked back around the corner just as another bomb exploded between the firemen's bunker and us, spraying shrapnel into the wall we crouched behind.

After we'd caught our breath, we started running again, wanting desperately to get away from the flames and explosions erupting all around us. We would run down a street that seemed to have been missed by the bombers and cower for a time in an archway or entrance, but soon more flames would shoot up in front of us. Fleeing the intense heat, we tried to move away from what seemed to be the main flight path of the bombers, but often we found the way blocked by a huge crater or a hillock of smouldering bricks and flaming wood that had toppled into the street. Sometimes we tried to pick our way over the debris, but often we gave up and turned back. Everywhere the bellowing wind drove the flames into a frenzy but the larger streets leading from the Alster lake were the worst.

Hot air and gases flew down these streets with incredible force, carrying everything that wasn't anchored towards the blazing incinerator that an hour or so earlier had been the districts of Hamm and Hammerbrook.

We found some partial shelter in a basement entrance but soon that, too, was ablaze. It was obvious that we couldn't stay where we were; pieces of the building had begun to fall on to the sidewalk. Despite the sustained roar of the wind and the sporadic explosions, I could sometimes hear the great cracking sounds made by the fire. I didn't see how we could avoid being crushed by the collapsing building if we stayed, or consumed by flames if we tried the street. I looked at Mother's face and read that she was undecided as to whether it would be worse to stay or leave. When there was a pause in the bombing, however, she wordlessly wrapped me like a mummy in my blanket. I could hardly breathe, and coughed miserably as she picked me up and edged back into the wind. By sticking close to walls and taking advantage of every possible windbreak, she eventually managed to get us both to a more sheltered side street.

We were both exhausted—limping, blistered, and bleeding from the ears and nose—when we stumbled into a shallow crater with some water at the bottom. The crater appeared to be in the small front garden of what had once been a handsome brick house with bays and turrets but was now a smouldering shambles. Mother thoroughly dampened her blanket and draped it over us. The terrible explosions seemed to have abated, although hundreds of incendiary bombs had fallen close by, some landing in rubble no more than a dozen yards away. A canister of liquid phosphorus had hit an office building just down the avenue. As the phosphorus burned and dripped its way through floor after floor, it looked as if the lights were being turned on one after the other by someone descending methodically through the building. Before the phosphorus reached the ground, flames were leaping from the windows of the upper floors.

Then a woman carrying an infant came running down the street along the same route we had taken. She was followed by a young man dressed in the khaki shorts and shirt of a Hitler Youth. I thought they must be fleeing from a bomb shelter that had been damaged, possibly the one Mother had been heading for when we first left our apartment building. The woman looked to be about Mother's age.

Her dress and her plaited pigtails appeared to have been burned, and she was almost completely naked below the waist. Despite his agile build and hiking shoes, the boy seemed to be having trouble keeping to his feet. I thought his difficulty might be the hot wind roaring down the avenue in front of us and almost expected to see him lifted up as he ran. Instead, after passing us at a gallop, he slowed to a grotesque caricature of walking, more like slow-motion skating, one leaden foot moving seconds after the other, with his arms spread out from his sides for balance. It took a while before I realized that both he and the woman were wading in molten asphalt. The woman slipped a couple of times and touched the pavement with one hand but managed to recover. Then she slowly fell head first towards the street, twisting at the last moment so that she landed on her back with the baby on her chest. The boy tried to reach her but slipped and fell, got up and fell again, and then again. Despite the incredible noise, I thought I could hear their screams and ducked down into the crater with my eyes closed and my hands over my ears.

Mother climbed to the edge of our crater and for a moment I worried that she was going to dash out to try to save the baby. But the hot wind burned her face and forced her back down. We lay in the crater beneath the blanket, getting hotter and hotter as the strong winds drove the flames into the sky. The image of the woman and the Hitler Youth writhing in hot asphalt remained vivid in the sweltering darkness until I realized that I was gasping for breath like a fish on land. No matter how deeply I inhaled, I couldn't get enough air into my lungs. When it seemed that I was about to suffocate, I pulled the blanket away and stuck up my head. Flaming logs and lumber, some of the planks several feet long, were sailing about in the air, along with millions and millions of sparks swirling at such speed they seemed to be tiny streaks of light. Without thinking, I opened my mouth wide and tried to suck in as much air as I could, until sharp needles of pain in my chest told me this was a bad mistake. I slumped back more terrified than ever. When I closed my eyes it felt like we were lying between railroad tracks while an endless train rumbled over us so swiftly that sparks from the wheels prickled my face.

I passed out for a time, awakening to find that breathing was still painful but that the explosions had stopped and the wind, though still almost as hot as steam, was not as strong. The heat was intense and so was our thirst, and we couldn't remain in the crater any longer without trying to drink the stinking water in the bottom. When we emerged we seemed to be in a winter snowstorm, with white flakes of ash flying in the wind. They looked so cool that I wanted to stick out my tongue to taste them, but there was still enough fire left in them to burn painfully. I'd lost my blanket but Mother wrapped us both in hers and we tried to walk so that the hot ashes were not blowing directly at us.

We hadn't progressed very far when we began to see bodies. Before leaving the area of the crater Mother had cautiously confirmed that the woman and her child and the Hitler Youth were dead, but she had shielded me from the sight. Although earlier we hadn't seen many other people in the streets, after the raid they seemed to be everywhere. Some, the obvious victims of exploding bombs, had been terribly torn and dismembered. Fire or heat had killed many more. Most were lying face down. The flames had shorn their hair and clothes, seared and swollen their buttocks, split their skin and raised their hips a few inches off the ground. Though unmistakably human, they looked like huge bratwursts. The smell of burnt flesh wrenched our stomachs and made us want to cry, but we hadn't enough water in us for tears or throwing up. Instead, I clasped Mother and buried my face into her dress.

Desperate for something to drink, we headed towards the Eilbek canal. Although we couldn't have been more than six or seven blocks away, it took us another hour to get there. Hundreds of people were still in the water, most of them near the opposite shore, where the canal was shallow, much shallower than usual because of the lack of rain during the past few months. Even more were on the banks, quite a few of them obviously dead. Some had faces as swollen and red as Chinese lanterns: their heads had been cooked while their bodies had been under water. Piteous moans, whimperings and cries of anguish rose from the canal. The screams of children seemed to hang in the air like paper kites. Now and then someone on the shore would start shrieking and jumping about and then they would leap into the water.

Normally, Hamburgers were extremely stoical. Sometimes they muttered curses or shouted insults, but typically they clamped their jaws and endured adversity in silence. That morning, they voiced their pain.

Listening to the voices in the water, I realized that they had been burned by phosphorus. Just as it burned through the floors of a building, it quickly penetrated living flesh and bone. Judging from the grotesque shapes and expressions of the dead, many had died in agony. Those still in the canal had discovered that the phosphorus became inactive when it was immersed but if they left the water it would start burning again as fiercely as before.

When another series of air-raid alarms announced that more bombers were within thirty minutes of Hamburg a spontaneous wailing and cursing arose from the sufferers, and then quickly subsided as if the effort had been too taxing or embarrassing. A few people started moving towards the church, whether to pray or to take shelter in the basement I couldn't say. Most, like us, remained by the canal. At the second alarm, signalling bombers within fifteen minutes, Mother recovered our blanket and wet it again in the canals and we were sitting with our feet in the water when the final siren announced that the bombers were overhead. The unexpected quickness of their arrival gave us hope. If the bombers were moving so much faster than expected, they were probably the smaller British Mosquitoes rather than Lancasters or American Flying Fortresses returning to pulverize whatever was still standing. We lay on the bank for roughly two hours, listening to an occasional Mosquito buzz across the sky to drop a few more bombs into the billowing smoke. Long before the all-clear sounded, Mother and I began to have stomach cramps and to vomit the canal water we had drunk earlier.

Where could we go? Brandsende, where Inge and my little sister, Renate, were staying, was impossible to reach because soldiers had cordoned off the streets near the City Hall. A rescue worker told us to go to the Stadtpark. There we would at least be safe from the fires and could try to get transportation out of the city. On our way we saw that the Karstadt department store had collapsed on its two air-raid shelters. People disinterred from the shelter reserved for store employees and city officials were dazed but unhurt, but rescue workers had taken hundreds of dead women and children from the other shelter and were bringing out more as we passed. Mother squeezed my hand to signal her relief that we had not been in the shelter of the dead.

There were thousands of refugees in the park by the time we got there: police and other city officials were loading people into every type of vehicle and sending them off without much enquiry into who was going where. Baby buggies and other paraphernalia stood where they'd been left; abandoned cats and dogs chased one another through the park.

I didn't think that Mother had decided to leave the city, but when a policeman herded us towards the back of a truck with a canvas cover she didn't pull away or resist. The truck driver demanded some money and answered her question about our destination with a single word: 'South!' And so we left the city. British fighters were reported to have strafed columns of fleeing refugees, and we stayed off the road the next day, parked in an orchard under trees laden with unripe apples to which we helped ourselves. I found swallowing painful but the tart flavour was heavenly. Mother and I took as many apples as we could carry and we still had some when we were dumped in the Bavarian village of Hof at around two in the morning. I was more asleep than awake as arrangements were made to stay in a room over a tavern beside a trout stream.

I can't remember much of the next few days other than the pain that came with breathing and eating, and that my mother was now my saviour, my beautiful hero. She had outwitted the Gestapo and faced down the Nazis in the shelter and everywhere else. She had held my hand and led me through exploding streets; she had never let go.

Then came news of my father. Mother told me she had talked to him on the telephone, that he'd arrived in Hamburg the day after we left and was staying with Inge in Brandsende. Though the British had made another massive raid on the city, Renate and Inge and her family had survived the bombs. Father arranged for us to hide on the farm of Marie Pimber, the woman who had been taking care of my middle sister, Helga, on the understanding that she was a Christian evacuee. Frau Pimber was part of a network of people, mainly communists or former communists, that Father called upon for Resistance assistance of one sort or another. Frau Pimber didn't much like the idea of hiding Jews, an offence for which she could be killed, but she had been childless until my sister arrived and had become so attached to her that she thought of Helga as her own. Faced with the prospect of losing Helga or letting us live on the farm, and offered as much material support as Father could muster, Frau Pimber agreed.

Two years passed. The war ended. A fortnight after the Allies formally accepted Germany's surrender on May 8, 1945, Father arrived at Frau Pimber's farm and we returned to Hamburg. My parents spent the next few months examining official and unofficial lists of survivors and waiting at railway stations for refugees to arrive. Father volunteered to help the British relief work among the refugees and displaced persons, pointing out that he was fluent in several languages and familiar with the cultures and countries from which many of the refugees had come. A British officer told him that he couldn't possibly be of any assistance because he was married to a Jew.

The joy of having escaped death made the unearthly ruins of Hamburg seem more like a smouldering paradise than the purgatory other people thought our once lovely city had become. After years of fear and hiding, I skipped down rubbled streets, flashing a smile and a thumbs-up at every British soldier I saw. I desperately wanted the British to know that I wasn't like the rest, that Winston Churchill was my hero, that I was glad they had come and that I wanted them to stay to protect the handful of Jews who had somehow survived.

The bombings had left me with such a fear of fire that my heart would begin to pound whenever I heard a siren, and something within me would shiver long after the sound died away. I was extremely uncomfortable in enclosed spaces and I dreaded elevators, tunnels, cellars and windowless rooms. I was also aware that thousands of Hamburg's children had been killed or maimed by the bombings, possibly even more than had been condemned to death for being Jews. And I hated all such killing with a passion that I couldn't always control.

At the same time I was glad that the intensive bombing of Hamburg by the British and the Americans during the summer of 1943 had enabled my mother and me to escape the fate of a death camp. Since we lived near the centre of the firestorm, the authorities who had ticketed us for Auschwitz assumed that we must have been among the thousands of the unrecognizable dead. Because our neighbours would not let us share their shelter I escaped being roasted alive. If the smile I flashed at British soldiers two years later sometimes appeared a trifle tight-lipped, that was because, while I wanted other Hamburgers to see how I felt, I was also afraid of what they might do when the Tommies packed their gear and went home.

Only a hundred or so Jews were left in Hamburg; another 17,000 had been killed or had fled.

Many Hamburgers must have felt some remorse for the suffering Germany had inflicted: when they saw, for example, pictures of the mountain of children's shoes at one of the death camps. That photograph made my father weep and place his large hand on my shoulder, while Mother had cried out and almost crushed Renate in her arms. But most people seemed too embittered by their own war experiences to give much thought to the suffering of others, especially of people whom they had been taught to hate. Every Hamburg family had experienced losses, most of them in the ten days of Operation Gomorrah, when somewhere between 45,000 and 70,000 civilians had died. Long after those raids, thousands of Hamburgers had to burrow beneath the rubble to sleep in cold cellars and basements. Whatever sparks of penitence smouldered beneath the ashes of the ruined city, the only expressions of regret I saw or heard in the streets, shops and schools of Hamburg were laments for the hardships of defeat. □

GRANTA

MILITARY LANDSCAPES
Simon Norfolk

The west coast of Scotland is one of the most intricate and beautiful landscapes in the world. Children, when asked to draw maps of Britain, usually depict it as a muddle of spikes and blobs reaching into the Atlantic. From the Solway Firth in the south to Cape Wrath in the north, estuaries and sea lochs bite far into the high and uneven ground of the mainland. Offshore lie 589 islands, as well as numerous rock islets and reefs. The largest and most westerly chain, the Outer Hebrides, provides a 150-mile-long barrier to the wind and seas which blow and swell, uninterrupted by land, all the way from North America. The barrier means that coastal waters are relatively sheltered. Glaciation has also made them remarkably deep. In the few miles between the island of Raasay and the mountains of Torridon the sea reaches down in places for more than 1,500 feet—the greatest sea depth off the British coast.

North of the Firth of Clyde there are very few towns or large villages, and none other than Oban and Stornoway of a scale that might support a medium-sized supermarket. The population of the Hebrides peaked in the census of 1841, but then came clearances and potato blight and the vanishing of the herring shoals. Large tracts of the west coast are empty, visible life confined to sea birds, seals, rabbits, deer, and the descendants of the sheep that Highland landlords exchanged for people (off to Glasgow and Canada) in the nineteenth century.

These conditions—deep water, few people on the land, plus easy access to Soviet navy routes—made the west coast of Scotland an ideal place to maintain, test and store all kinds of weaponry during the Cold War, and to continue a technical, military history that began a hundred years ago with torpedo ranges in the Clyde's sea lochs and anthrax trials which poisoned the island of Gruinard (the plan, 'Operation Vegetarian', was to wipe out Germany's cow population by bombing them with anthrax-infected cattle feed).

Today, the Scottish west coast continues to be the most heavily armed region of Britain and quite possibly Europe, offering mountains and glens for low-flying fighter and bomber exercises, sea and moorland for uranium-depleted artillery fire, underground storage for nuclear weapons and naval fuel, emergency moorings for nuclear submarines. I go there every summer. The loveliness of the changing light on sea and mountain makes it hard to imagine the ominous technology buried beneath.   *Ian Jack*

Opposite: an RAF Tornado over the Cape Wrath firing range

1. The missile
testing range,
South Uist,
Outer Hebrides

2. The Lochmaddy
Submarine Exercise Area,
from the Isle of Scalpay

3. Impact zone,
naval and aerial
bombardment
range, Cape Wrath

4. The 'Perisher' submarine-commander exercise area, between Ayrshire and Arran

5. A member of the RAF regiment during the 'Neptune Warrior 06' military exercise, Loch Ewe

6. The bomb testing range at Luce Bay, in Galloway

7. HMS 'Richmond' undergoing sound signature testing on Loch Goil

8. Petroleum, Oil, Lubricants (POL) store, near Faslane, on the Gare Loch

9. The Dundrennan tank firing range, near Kirkcudbright on the Solway Firth

10. Rhu Marina, on the Gare Loch, near Faslane, the main base for Britain's nuclear submarines

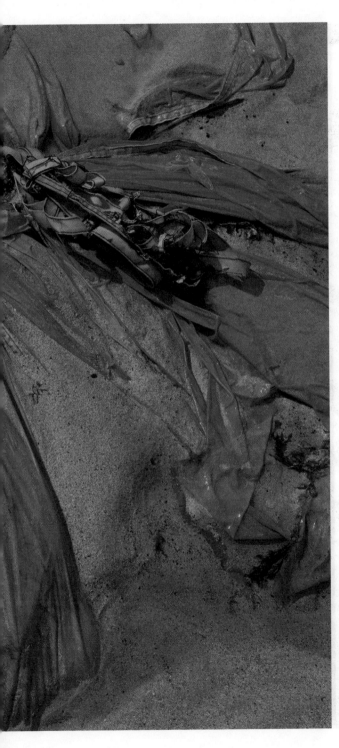

11. A retarder parachute from a missile or a 'drone', on the missile test range on South Uist

12. The 'Z' Berth for nuclear submarines, off Rothesay, Isle of Bute

13. The view over Loch Long to Royal Naval Armaments Depot (RNAD) Coulport, where nuclear weapons are stored

14. The 'GIUK Gap', north-west of the Butt of Lewis, where hydrophone networks on the sea bed listen for submarines

15. Bosnian-style 'Skills House' for Fighting in Built-Up Areas ('FIBUA') close-combat training

16. Warning against dumped munitions in Portpatrick, near Stranraer

The pictures in more detail

1. The missile testing range on South Uist, now run by the Anglo-American defence company QinetiQ, was set up in the 1950s to test the Corporal nuclear missile system bought from the USA. It is one of the busiest such ranges in the world, and one of the longest, stretching far into the Atlantic. In a secret report from 1981, declassified in 2002, the Naval Radiation Protection Services (NRPS) discovered that between 1967 and 1980 the launching site and surrounding area had been contaminated by large amounts of Cobalt-60, a radioisotope sprayed from the back of moving missiles to help radar track them. The report concluded that 'both the ammunition technicians at RA Range Hebrides and possibly the general public were being placed at unnecessary radiological risk'. An earlier investigation in 2002 found that 352 drums of waste from the decontamination process were buried at the range.

2. Most submarine exercises in the UK take place off the west coast of Scotland. Following the sinking of the trawler *Antares* by the submarine *Trenchant* in 1990, a system called 'Subfacts' was introduced. This divides the seas off the west of Scotland into 'Submarine Exercise Areas' (SEAs) and a daily broadcast tells fishermen which to avoid. In November 2002, the nuclear-powered submarine *Trafalgar* crashed into the Isle of Skye at fifteen knots and a depth of fifty metres while practising torpedo evasion tactics.

3. The most north-westerly point on the British mainland is an 8,400-acre weapons range and army exercise area. Cape Wrath (a Norse word for 'turning point') has the highest sea cliffs on mainland Britain. The Naval Gunfire Support Range is used by Royal Navy and other NATO vessels as a practise area for 4.5-inch and 5-inch guns. The cliffs, an important nesting ground for birds, rise to almost 1,000 feet and are used as ranging marks for the guns. Nearby Garvie Island is the only place in Europe where aircraft can drop live 1,000lb bombs. Cape Wrath assumed greater importance when US ships lost access to ranges in Puerto Rico in 1999 after a civilian was accidentally killed.

4. In November 1990, the nuclear-powered attack submarine *Trenchant* caught the Kintyre-based trawler *Antares'* nets and dragged

her to the bottom of the Arran Trench, between the Isle of Arran and the mainland. All four crew of the *Antares* drowned. Among the submarine crew were officers reaching the end of the six-week 'Perisher' submarine commanders' course. The subsequent inquiry blamed 'partial breakdown in the watchkeeping structure and standards' on board *Trenchant*.

5. Every summer, aircraft, surface ships and submarines in the west of Scotland are brought together for the 'Neptune Warrior' war game. Elaborate scenarios written by military planners test the preparedness of officers and men. These might be exercises in 'conventional warfare', a terrorist attack by patrol boats, 'Bosnian enclave'-type situations, or even how to deal with troublesome members of the press.

6. Luce Bay is a QinetiQ-owned testing range for weapons launched from jets and helicopters. Damage to the marine environment from bombing exercises is such that the sea bed has been fitted with special mattresses to absorb the explosions. The bay is also used for NATO training exercises. In September 2003, a NATO exercise named 'Northern Light' practised a large-scale amphibious landing employing around fifty ships and submarines and thirty-four aircraft.

7. The Defence Evaluation and Research Agency's Noise Range at Loch Goil can provide sound analysis of all the systems on a ship or submarine. The loch, which is deep and quiet, is lined with hydrophones which map the unique sound signature of a vessel. *Richmond*, a Type 23 'Duke'-class frigate, entered service in 1995. Primarily an anti-submarine frigate, her diesel, electric and gas turbine combination engine is capable of near-silent running. Her computer-assisted sonar, sensor and communications equipment has recently been upgraded, necessitating the retesting of her sound signature.

8. This is one of many fuel stores which hold hundreds of thousands of tons of petroleum under Scotland's glens. In addition to the nuclear-powered and nuclear-armed Trident fleet, Faslane also houses five conventionally armed Swiftsure-class nuclear submarines, ships of the Third Mine Countermeasures Squadron and the Northern Ireland Squadron. In 2001, Commachio Company of the Royal Marines was

transferred to Faslane to protect the submarine fleet. Faslane will also house the new Astute-class submarines and Trident's replacement.

9. The armament testing range at Dundrennan near Kirkcudbright covers 4,500 acres and its danger zone extends over 120 square miles of the Solway Firth. Since 1982, more than 6,000 depleted uranium shells, usually in the form of anti-tank munitions, have been fired from the range into the Solway Firth. Most of the twenty tons of shells remain on the sea bed. Depleted uranium has a half-life of 4.5 billion years. Dundrennan is also the planned site for controversial electro-magentic 'super-gun' trials on behalf of the US military. The gun is able to hurl a projectile at 7,500 mph, more than five times the top speed of Concorde. Each shell will be about a foot long and as narrow as a broom handle. The kinetic force with which it hits its target will be so great that it is unlikely to require any explosive warhead.

10. Faslane, the base for the Trident submarine fleet, employs 7,000 people and stretches along the banks of the Gare Loch behind razor wire, guarded by armed police and infrared cameras. At the mouth of the loch is the 'degaussing range' at Rosneath, where submarines are demagnetized to ensure they do not trigger floating mines.

11. The first surface-to-air missiles were aimed at towed targets dragged on a four-mile cable behind an RAF bomber. More recently tests of the Advanced Medium Range Air to Air Missile (AMRAAM) to be fitted to the new Eurofighter have used target drones such as the Banshee 400. These small unmanned jets can be tracked by radar or heat-seeking missiles and programmed to mimic the evasive tactics of enemy aircraft. Although most of the test material ends up in the Atlantic, some military detritus can be found around the site.

12. A 'Z' Berth is a jetty or mooring buoy for nuclear submarines in case of emergencies. Scotland has five. When plans for the 'Z' Berth in Loch Ewe were discovered, all 500 residents around the loch were issued with potassium iodate tablets as a precautionary measure.

13. The 200-odd warheads that comprise Britain's nuclear deterrent are stored in air-locked vaults behind concrete and steel blast doors

buried in the hillside at Coulport, twenty-seven miles from Glasgow.

14. The Greenland-Iceland-UK Gap was a key battleground in the Cold War. Soviet submarines based at the pens on the Kola peninsula had to pass through the gap before going on patrols around the world and could be detected and tailed. The US took responsibility for the Greenland to Iceland sector, the UK for the rest. The primary defence from the 1970s on was SOSUS, a system of underwater hydrophones strung out at depth across the ocean, which was said to be able to hear a submarine 1,100 miles away and pinpoint its location to an area of ten square miles.

15. Due to lessons learned during the war in Northern Ireland, Fighting In Built-Up Areas (FIBUA) is a speciality of the British Army. Mock 'Belfast' villages exist in Germany and Norfolk and a full-sized Bosnian village has been built on Salisbury Plain.

16. Portpatrick, on the Scottish mainland, overlooks the narrow channel between Scotland and Northern Ireland. At its deepest point is a long trench, Beaufort Dyke, which was used for dumping munitions and radioactive waste after the Second World War. An estimated 1.7 million tonnes of weapons including artillery shells, phosphorous flares, mortars, incendiaries and cluster bombs have been jettisoned off boats, supposedly into the dyke. Two tonnes of low- and medium-level radioactive waste have been added to the Irish Sea by private companies, including the defence contractor Ferranti. Around 14,000 tonnes of phosgene-charged rockets were also dumped into Beaufort Dyke. Phosgene was used by both the Germans and the Allies. It is a colourless poison gas, designed to incapacitate rather than to kill, which acts as an acute respiratory irritant, causing severe lung damage. In 1995, 4,000 phosphorous incendiary bombs were washed up on Mull, Oban, Arran and other parts of Scotland's west coast. A British Gas pipeline had been laid through the heart of the dump and its trenching machine dispersed thousands of shells. Subsequent enquiries found that bombs had been dumped well short of the intended site, some only three miles offshore in as little as fifty metres of water.   □

GRANTA

TOKYO YEAR ZERO
David Peace

'*D*etective Minami! Detective Minami! Detective Minami!'
I open my eyes. *From dreams that are not my own.* I sit up in my chair at my desk. *Dreams I do not want.* My collar is wet and my whole suit damp. My hair itches. My skin itches—
'Detective Minami! Detective Minami!'
Detective Nishi is taking down the blackout curtains, bright warm shafts of dawn and dust filling the office as the sun rises up beyond the tape-crossed windows—
'Detective Minami!'
'Did you just say something?' I ask Nishi—
Nishi shakes his head. Nishi says, 'No.'
I stare up at the ceiling. Nothing moves in the bright light. The fans have stopped. No electricity. The telephones silent. No lines. The toilets blocked. No water. Nothing—
'Kumagaya was hit during the night,' says Nishi. 'There are reports of gunfire from the palace…'
'I didn't dream it, then?'
I take out my handkerchief. It is old and it is dirty. I wipe my neck again. Then I wipe my face. Now I check my pockets—
They are handing out potassium cyanide to the women, the children and the aged, saying this latest cabinet reshuffle foretells the end of the war, the end of Japan, the end of the world…
Nishi holds up a small box and asks, 'You looking for these?'
I snatch the box of Muronal out of his hands. I check the contents. *Enough.* I stuff the box back into my jacket pocket—
Sirens and warnings all through the night; Tokyo hot and dark, hidden and cowed; night and day, rumours of new weapons, fears of new bombs; first Hiroshima, then Nagasaki, next is Tokyo…
Bombs that mean the end of Japan, the end of the world…
No sleep. Only dreams. No sleep. Only dreams…
Night and day, this is why I take these pills…
This is what I tell myself, night and day…
'They were on the floor,' says Nishi—
I nod. I ask, 'You got a cigarette?'
Nishi shakes his head. *I curse him.* There are five more days until the next special ration. *Five more days…*
The office door swings open—
Detective Fujita storms into the room. Detective Fujita has a *Police*

Bulletin in his hand. Fujita says, 'Sorry, more bad news...'

He tosses the bulletin on to my desk. Nishi picks it up—

Nishi is young. Nishi is keen. Too young...

'It's from the Shinagawa Police Station,' he says, and reads, 'Body discovered in suspicious circumstances at the Women's Dormitory Building of the Dai-Ichi Naval Clothing Department...'

'Just a moment,' I tell him. 'Surely anything to do with the Naval Clothing Department falls under the jurisdiction of the *Kempeitai*? This is a case for the Military Police, not civilian...'

'I know,' says Fujita. 'But Shinagawa are requesting Murder Squad detectives. Like I say, I'm really sorry I pulled it...'

No one wants a case. Not today. Not now...

I get up from my desk. I grab my hat—

'Come on,' I tell Fujita and Nishi. 'We'll find someone else. We'll dump the case. You just watch me...'

I go out of our room and down the main hallway of the First Investigative Division of the Tokyo Metropolitan Police Department; down Police Arcade, room to room, office to office, door to door—

Door to door. *No one.* Office to office. *No one.* Room to room. *No one.* Everyone evacuated or absent—

No one wants a case. Not today...

Just Fujita, Nishi and me now—

I curse. I curse. I curse...

I stand in the corridor. I ask Nishi, 'Where's Chief Kita?'

'All chiefs were summoned to a meeting at seven a.m....'

I take out my pocket watch. It's already past eight—

'Seven a.m.?' I repeat. 'Maybe today is the day, then?'

'Didn't you hear the nine o'clock news last night?' he asks. 'There's to be an imperial broadcast at noon today...'

I eat acorns. I eat leaves. I eat weeds...

'A broadcast about what?'

'I don't know, but the entire nation has been instructed to find a radio so that they can listen to it...'

'Today *is* the day, then,' I say. 'People, return to your homes! Kill your children! Kill your wives! Then kill yourself!'

'No, no, no,' says Nishi—

Too young. Too keen...

'If we're going to go,' interrupts Fujita, 'let's at least go via

Shimbashi and get some cigarettes...'

'That's a very good idea,' I say. 'No cars for us anyway...'

'Let's take the Yamate Line round to Shinagawa,' he says. 'Take our time, walk slowly, and hope we're too late...'

'If the Yamate Line is even running,' I remind him—

'Like I say,' says Fujita again, 'take our time.'

Detective Fujita, Nishi and I walk down the stairs, through the doors, and leave headquarters by the back way, on the side of the building that faces away from the grounds of the Imperial Palace—

That looks out on the ruins of the Ministry of Justice.

The shortest route to Shimbashi from Sakuradamon is through the Hibiya Park, through this park that is now no park—

Black winter trees in the white summer heat...

'Even if we are routed in battle,' Nishi is saying. 'The mountains and the rivers remain. The people remain...'

Plinths without statues, posts with no gates...

'The hero Kusunoki pledged to live and die seven times in order to save Japan,' he states. 'We can do no less...'

No foliage. No bushes. No grass now...

'We must fight on,' he urges. 'Even if we have to chew the grass, eat the earth and live in the fields.'

Just stark black winter trees...

'With our broken swords and our exhausted arrows,' I say. 'Our hearts burned by fire, eaten by tears.'

In the white summer heat...

Nishi smiling. 'Exactly.'

The white heat...

Nishi in one ear and now the harsh noise of martial music from a sound-truck in the other as we leave the park that is no park, down streets that are no streets, past buildings that are no buildings—

'Oh, so bravely, off to Victory / In so far as we have vowed and left our land behind...'

Buildings of which nothing remains but their front walls; now only sky where their windows and ceilings should be—

'Who can die without first having shown his true mettle / Each time I hear the bugles of our advancing army...'

The dates on which these buildings ceased to be buildings

witnessed in the height of the weeds that sprout here and there among the black mountains of shattered brick—

'I close my eyes and see wave upon wave of flags cheering us into battle...'

The shattered brick, the lone chimneys and the metal safes that crashed down through the floors as these buildings went up in flames, night after night—

'The earth and its flora burn in flames / As we endlessly part the plains...'

Night after night, from the eleventh month of last year, siren after siren, bomb after bomb—

'Helmets emblazoned with the Rising Sun / And, stroking the mane of our horses...'

Bomb after bomb, fire after fire, building after building, neighbourhood after neighbourhood, until there are no buildings, there are no neighbourhoods and there is no city, no Tokyo—

'Who knows what tomorrow will bring—life?'

Only the survivors now—

'Or death in battle?'

Hiding under the rubble, living among the ruins, three or four families to a shack of rusted iron and salvaged wood, or in the railroad or the subway stations—

The lucky ones...

'We must fight on,' repeats Detective Nishi. 'For if we do not fight on, the Emperor himself will be executed and the women of Japan will be subjected to methodical rape so that the next Japanese will not be Japanese...'

I curse him...

Beneath telegraph poles that stand as grave markers, down these streets that are no streets, we walk as Nishi rants on—

'In the mountains of Nagano, we shall make our final stand; on Maizuruyama, on Minakamiyama, on Zozan!'

There are people on these streets that are no streets now, people that are no people; exhausted ghosts in early-morning queues, bitter-enders waiting for lunches outside hodgepodge dining halls in old movie theatres, their posters replaced by slogans—

'We Are All Soldiers on the Home Front...'

The sound-truck has gone and with it that song we have heard every day for the last seven years, 'Roei no Uta'—

Just the noise of Nishi's voice now—

'Every man under sixty-five, every woman under forty-five will take up a bamboo spear and march off...

'To defend our beloved Japan...'

I stop in the middle of this street that is no street and I grab Nishi by the collar of his civil defence uniform and I push him up against a scorched wall, a scorched wall on which is written—

Let Us All Help One Another with Smiling Faces...'

'Go back to headquarters, Detective,' I tell him—

He blinks, open-mouthed, and now he nods—

I pull him back from the black wall—

'I want to make sure one of us, at least, is able to hear this imperial broadcast,' I tell him. 'You can then report what was said, if Fujita and I are unable to hear it...'

I let go of his collar—

Nishi nods again.

'Dismissed,' I shout now, and Nishi stands to attention, salutes and then he bows—

And he leaves.

'Thank you very much,' laughs Detective Fujita.

'Nishi is very young,' I tell him.

'Young and very keen...'

'Yes,' I say. 'But I don't think he'd be too keen on our old friend Matsuda Giichi...'

'Very true,' laughs Fujita again as we walk on, on down these streets that are no streets, past buildings that are no buildings—

In this city that is no city.

To Shimbashi, Tokyo. There are lines of soldiers unloading wooden crates from two Imperial Army trucks outside the temporary offices of Matsuda Giichi and his affiliates in an open lot near the back of the Shimbashi Railway Station; Matsuda Giichi himself giving the orders—

'Sellers and Buyers Are All Comrades in Arms...'

Matsuda Giichi in a new silk suit, stood on a crate with a Panama hat in one hand and a foreign cigar in the other—

The brand new Emperor of Tokyo...

Matsuda smiles when he sees Fujita and me—

David Peace

The only man smiling in Tokyo...
'I thought you lot had all run off to the mountains,' he laughs.
'The last stand of the Japanese race and all that...'
'What's in the crates?' I ask him—
'Ever the detective, aren't you?' says Matsuda. 'But you two might want to start thinking of changing your line of work...'
'What's in the crates?' I ask again—
'Army helmets,' he says—
'Not thinking of joining the war effort, are you?'
'Little late for that,' he says. 'Anyway, I did my bit on the continent—not that anyone ever thanked me for my trouble. But, past is past, now I'm going to help this country get back on its feet...'
'Very patriotic of you,' I say. 'But we've not lost yet.'
Matsuda looks at his watch, his new foreign watch, and nods. 'Not yet, you're quite right, Detective. But have you seen all those columns of smoke rising from all those government buildings...?'
Both Detective Fujita and I shake our heads—
'Well, that means they're burning all their documents and their records. That's the smoke of surrender...'
'The smoke of defeat.'
Two more army trucks pull up. Horns sound. Matsuda says, 'Now, I am very sorry to be rude but, as you gentlemen can see, today is a very busy day. So was there anything you specifically wanted? Like a new job? A new name? A new life? A new past...?'
'Just cigarettes,' say Fujita and I simultaneously.
'Go see Senju,' says Matsuda Giichi.
Both Fujita and I thank him—
'Senju's round the back.'
Fujita and I bow to him—
And curse him.
Detective Fujita and I walk round the back of Matsuda's temporary office to his makeshift warehouse and his lieutenant—
Senju Akira stripped to his waist, a sheathed short sword in his right hand, as he supervises the unloading of another truck—
Its boxes of Imperial Chrysanthemum cigarettes—
I ask, 'Where did you get hold of all these?'
'Never ask a policeman,' laughs Senju. 'Look, those in the know, know, and those who don't, don't...'

'So what's with your boss and all those helmets?' I ask him.

'What goes around, comes around,' smiles Senju again. 'We sold the army saucepans to make helmets, now they're selling us helmets to make saucepans...'

'Well then, you can sell us on some of those Chrysanthemum cigarettes,' says Fujita.

'Don't tell me you've actually got hard cash,' says Senju.

Detective Fujita and I both shake our heads again—

'Fucking cops,' sighs Senju Akira as he hands us each five packs of cigarettes. 'Worse than thieves...'

We thank him and we bow to him—

And we curse him and curse him...

We share a match in the shade—

In the shade that is no shade...

We smoke, then we walk on.

There are uniformed police officers on duty at Shimbashi Railway Station, checking packages and bundles for contraband—

Knapsacks and pockets for black-market cigarettes—

Detective Fujita and I take out our police notebooks and identify ourselves at the gate—

The station and the platform are almost deserted, the Yamate Line train almost empty—

The sun is climbing, the temperature rising. I wipe my neck and I wipe my face—

I itch—

I itch as I stare out of the windows; the elevated tracks of the Yamate Line now the highest points left in most of Tokyo, a sea of rubble in all directions except to the east—

The docks and the other, real sea.

The uniforms behind the desk at Shinagawa Police Station are expecting us; two waiting to lead us down to the docks—

One called Uchida, the other Murota—

To the scene of the crime...

'They think it might be a woman called Miyazaki Mitsuko,' they tell us as we walk, panting and sweating like dogs in the sun. 'This Miyazaki girl was originally from Nagasaki and had been brought

up to Tokyo just to work in the Naval Clothing Department and so
she was living in the workers' dormitory...'

The sun beating down on our hats...

'Back in May, she was given leave to return home to visit her
family in Nagasaki. However, she never arrived in Nagasaki and never
returned to work or the dormitory...'

The neighbourhood stinks...

'Most of the workers have actually moved out of the dormitory
now as the factory of the Naval Clothing Department is no longer
in operation. However, there have been a number of thefts from the
buildings and so the caretaker and his assistant were searching and
then securing the premises...'

It stinks of oil and shit...

'They went down into one of the air-raid shelters, one that has
not been used in a while, and that was when they...'

It stinks of retreat...

'Found the naked body of a woman...'

Surrender...

This neighbourhood of factories and their dormitories, factories
geared to the war effort, dormitories occupied by volunteer workers;
the factories bombed and the dormitories evacuated, any buildings
still standing now stained black and stripped empty—

This is the scene of the crime...

The Women's Dormitory Building of the Dai-Ichi Naval Clothing
Department still standing, next to a factory where only the broken
columns and the gateposts remain—

No equipment and no parts—

The workers have fled—

This is the scene...

Two men sit motionless before the abandoned dormitory,
sheltering from the sun in the shadow of some cabin-cum-office—

'I really can't understand it,' the older man is saying. 'I really can't
understand it. I really can't understand it at all...'

The older man is the caretaker of the dormitory. The other,
younger man is the boiler-man. It was the boiler-man who found the
body and it is the boiler-man who now points at the two corrugated-
metal doors to an air-raid shelter and says, 'She's down there...In a
cupboard at the back of the shelter.

The sun beating down on our hats...

I pull back the two corrugated-tin doors and then immediately I step back again. The smell of human waste is overwhelming—

Human piss. Human shit. Human piss. Human shit...

Three steps down, the floor of the shelter is water—

Not rain or sea water, the shelter has flooded with sewage from broken pipes; a black sunken pool of piss and shit—

'We could do with Nishi now,' says Fujita.

I turn back to the caretaker in his shade—

'When did this happen?' I ask him—

'In the May air raids,' he says.

'How did you find the body, then?' I ask the boiler-man—

'With this,' he replies, and holds up an electric torch.

'Pass it over here,' I tell the man—

The boiler-man gets to his feet, mumbling about batteries, and brings the torch over to Fujita and me—

I snatch it from him.

I take out my handkerchief. I put it over my nose and my mouth. I peer back down the steps—

I switch on the torch—

I shine the light across the black pool of sewage water, the water about a metre deep, furniture sticking up here and there out of the pool. Against the furthest wall a wardrobe door hangs open—

She is down here. She is down here. She is down here...

I switch off the torch. I turn back from the hole. I take off my boots. I take off my socks. I start to unbutton my shirt—

'You're never going in there, are you?' asks the caretaker.

'That was my question too,' laughs Fujita—

I unbutton my trousers. I take them off—

'There are rats down there,' says the caretaker. 'And that water's poisonous. A bite or a cut and you'll be...'

I say, 'But she's not going to walk out of there, is she?'

Fujita starts to unbutton his shirt now, cursing—

'Just another corpse,' he says—

'You two as well,' I say to the two uniforms from Shinagawa. 'One of you inside, one of you holding these doors open...'

I tie my dirty handkerchief tight around my face—

I put my boots back on. I pick up the torch—

David Peace

Now one, two, three steps down I go—
Fujita behind me, still cursing—
'Nishi back in the office...'
I can feel the floor of the shelter beneath the water, the water up
to my knees. I can hear the mosquitoes and I can sense the rats—
The water up to my waist, I wade towards the wardrobe—
My boots slip beneath the water, my legs stumble—
My knee bangs into the corner of a table—
I pray for a bruise, a bruise not a cut—
I reach the far side of the shelter—
I reach the wardrobe doors—
She is in here. In here...
I glimpse her as I pull at the doors, but the doors are stuck,
submerged furniture trapping her in, closing the doors—
Detective Fujita holds the torch as the uniformed officer and I
clear the chairs and the tables away, piece by piece—
Piece by piece until the doors swing open—
The doors swing open and, *she is here...*
The body bloated in places, punctured in others—
Pieces of flesh here, but only bones there—
Her hair hangs down across her skull—
Teeth parted as though to speak—
To whisper, *I am here...*
Now the uniform holds the torch as Fujita and I take the body
between us, *cold here*, as we carry and then hoist it out of the black
water, *warm there*, up the dank steps, *hard here*, out—
Out into the air, *soft there*, out into the sun—
Panting and sweating like dogs...
Fujita, the uniform and I flat on our backs in the dirt, the badly
decomposed and naked body of a young woman between us—
Bloated, punctured, flesh and bones, hair and teeth...
I use my jacket to wipe myself, to dry myself—
I smoke a Chrysanthemum cigarette—
Now I turn to the two men sat in the shade, the caretaker and
the boiler-man, and I say, 'You told these officers that you think this
might be the body of a Miyazaki Mitsuko...'
Flesh and bones, hair and teeth...
The caretaker nods his head.

144

'Why did you say that?' I ask him. 'Why do you think that?'

'Well, it was always a bit strange,' he says. 'The way she left and never came back. Never went home and never came back here...'

'But thousands of people have gone missing,' says Fujita. 'Who knows how many people have been killed in the raids?'

'Yes,' says the caretaker. 'But she left after the first raids on this place and she never arrived back in Nagasaki...'

'Who says so?' I ask him. 'Her parents?'

'They might have been lying,' says Fujita. 'To keep their daughter from coming back to Tokyo...'

The caretaker shrugs. The caretaker says, 'Well, if she did get back to Nagasaki, she's as good as dead anyway...'

I finish my cigarette. I nod at the body in the dirt. 'Is there any way you could identify this as her?'

The caretaker looks at the remains of the corpse on the ground. He looks away again. He shakes his head—

'Not like that,' he says. 'All I remember is that she had a watch with her name engraved on its back. It was a present from her father when she moved to Tokyo. Very proud of it she was...'

Fujita puts his handkerchief back over his mouth—

He crouches down again. He shakes his head—

There's no watch on the wrist of this corpse—

I nod back towards the air-raid shelter and say to Detective Fujita, 'It might still be down there somewhere...'

'Yes,' he says. 'And it might not be.'

'How about you?' I ask the boiler-man. 'Did you know her?'

The boiler-man shakes his head. He says, 'Before my time.'

'He only started here this June,' says the caretaker. 'And Miyazaki was last seen around here at the end of May.'

I ask, 'Can you remember the exact dates?'

He tilts his head to one side. He closes his eyes. He screws them up tight. Then he opens his eyes again and shakes his head—

'I'm sorry,' he says, 'but I lose track of the time...'

I can hear an engine now. I can hear a Jeep...

I turn around as the vehicle approaches—

It is a Military Police vehicle—

It is the *Kempeitai*.

The Jeep stops and two *Kempei* officers get out of the front, both

145

wearing side-arms and swords. They are accompanied by two older men sporting the armbands of the Neighbourhood Association—

I want to applaud them. *The Kempeitai.* I want to cheer—

No one wants a case. Not today. Not now…

This body was found on military property; this is their property, this is their body, this is their case.

Detective Fujita and I step forward. Fujita and I bow deeply—

These two Kempei *officers look very much like Fujita and I; the older man is in his late forties, the other in his late thirties…*

Detective Fujita and I introduce ourselves to them—

I am looking in a mirror. I am looking at myself…

We apologize for being on military property—

But they are the soldiers, we're just police…

There are briefer reciprocal bows—

This is their city, their year…

The younger officer introduces the older man as Captain Muto and himself as Corporal Katayama—

I am looking in a mirror…

I bow again and now I make my report to the two *Kempei* officers, the two men from the Neighbourhood Association still standing close enough to hear what I am telling them—

The times and dates. Places and names…

I finish my report and I bow again—

They glance at their watches.

Now Captain Muto, the older of the two *Kempei* officers, walks over to the corpse stretched out in the dust. He stands and he stares at the body for a while before turning back to Fujita and me—

'We will need an ambulance from the Keio University Hospital to transport this body to the hospital. We will need Dr Nakadate of Keio to perform the autopsy on the body…'

Detective Fujita and I both nod—

This is their body, their case…

But Captain Muto turns to the two uniforms now and says, 'You two men return to Shinagawa and request that the Keio University Hospital send an ambulance immediately and that Dr Nakadate is made available to perform the autopsy.'

Uchida and Murota, the two uniforms, both nod, salute and then bow deeply to the *Kempei* man—

Fujita and I both curse—

No escape now...

Now Captain Muto gestures at the caretaker and then the boiler-man and asks us, 'Which of these men work here?'

'They both do,' I reply.

Captain Muto points to the boiler-man and shouts, 'Boiler-man, you go get a blanket or something similar and as many old newspapers as you can find. And do it quickly as well!'

The boiler-man runs off inside the building.

The older *Kempei* officer glances at his watch again and now he asks the caretaker, 'Do you have a radio here?'

'Yes,' he nods. 'In our cabin.'

'There is to be an imperial broadcast shortly and every citizen of Japan has been ordered to listen to this broadcast. Go now and check that your radio is tuned correctly and in full working order.'

The caretaker nods. The caretaker bows. The caretaker goes off to his cabin, passing the boiler-man as he returns with a coarse grey blanket and a bundle of old newspapers—

The younger *Kempei* man now turns to Fujita and me and tells us, 'Lay that body out on these newspapers and then cover it with this blanket ready for the ambulance...'

Fujita and I tie our handkerchiefs back over our mouths and our noses and set to work, laying the newspapers and then the body out, partially covering it with the blanket—

This is not our case any more...

But now the boiler-man nervously approaches the younger of the *Kempei* officers. The boiler-man's head is bent low in apology, first mumbling and then nodding, pointing here and there in answer to the questions the officer is asking—

The conversation ends.

Corporal Katayama strides over to his senior colleague and says, 'This man says there have been a number of thefts from our property and that he suspects these robberies to have been committed by the Korean labourers billeted in that building over there...'

The younger *Kempei* man is pointing to a scorched three-storey building on the opposite side of the dormitory—

'Are these workers under any kind of supervision?' asks the older man. 'Or are they just free to come and go?'

'I heard that they were under guard until the end of May,' says the boiler-man. 'Then the younger and stronger ones were taken to work in the north but the older, weaker ones were left here.'

'And do they do any kind of work?'

'They are meant to help us with the repairs to the buildings but either they are too sick or there are not enough materials available, so usually they just stay in there…'

Captain Muto, the older *Kempei* officer, who still keeps looking at his watch, now abruptly waves at all of the surrounding buildings and shouts, 'I want all these buildings searched!'

Fujita and I have finished laying out the body on the newspapers. Now I glance at Fujita. I am not sure if Captain Muto means for us to search or not. Fujita doesn't move—

But now the *Kempei* captain barks—

'You two, take this dormitory!'

This is not our case any more…

Fujita and I both salute him. Fujita and I both bow to him. Then we march off into the building—

I am cursing. Fujita cursing…

'Nishi back in the office…'

Detective Fujita takes the top floor. I take the second floor. The knotted wooden floorboards of the corridor squeak. *Knock-knock.* Door to door. Room to room. Every room exactly the same—

The tatami mats, frayed and well worn. The single window and the blackout curtain. The thin green walls and the chrysanthemum wallpaper, limp and peeling—

Every room empty, abandoned.

The very end of the corridor. The very last room. The very last door. *Knock-knock.* I turn the handle. I open the door—

The same old mats. The single window. The same blackout curtain. The thin walls. The same peeling paper—

In another empty room.

I walk across the mats. I pull back the curtain. The sunlight illuminates a partially burnt mosquito coil on a low table—

The stench of piss. The stench of shit—

Human piss and human shit…

I open the closet built into the wall and there, among a heap of bedding, crouches an old man, his face buried in a *futon*—

I crouch down. I say, 'Don't be afraid...'

Now he turns his head from the bedding and looks up at me; the old man's face is flat and his lips are chapped and parted, showing broken yellow dirt-flecked teeth—

He stinks of piss and of shit—

The old man is a Korean—

I curse and I curse...

He is a *Yobo*—

'Congratulations!'

I look round; Corporal Katayama, the younger *Kempei* officer, is stood in the doorway, Fujita behind him, shaking his head—

'Bring him downstairs!' orders the *Kempei* man—

I stare at this Corporal Katayama—

I am looking into a mirror...

'Quickly!' he barks.

The old man buries his head back in the bedding, his shoulders shaking, mumbling and moaning—

'I didn't do anything! Please...'

His breath foul and rotten—

I take him by his shoulders and start to pull him from the bedding, from the closet, the old man wriggling and struggling—

'I didn't do anything! Please, I want to live!'

'Help him!' the corporal orders Fujita—

Fujita and I drag the old man from the closet, from the room, by his shoulders, by his arms, then out into the corridor, back along the floorboards; we have an arm each now—

The man's trunk and legs aslant—

His feet are trailing—

The *Kempei* officer marching behind with his sword in one hand, kicking at the soles of the old man's feet, striking him with his sword to hurry him along—

Down the stairs—

Into the light...

'That's *him*!' cries the boiler-man now. 'That's him!'

'Get me two spades now!' shouts the older *Kempei* officer, and the caretaker runs back inside his cabin-cum-office—

'You two, bring the suspect over here.'

Fujita and I march the old Korean man over to Captain Muto in the shade of the other dormitory—

Into the shadows…

The caretaker comes back with the two spades. Captain Muto takes one of the spades from the caretaker and hands it to the boiler-man. He nods at a patch of ground that might once have been a flowerbed, then perhaps a vegetable patch, but now is nothing but hard, packed soil stained black—

'Dig a hole,' he says.

The caretaker and the boiler-man begin to dig up the ground, the caretaker already sweating and saying, 'He made a peephole to spy on the women workers as they bathed…'

The boiler-man wiping his skull, then his neck and agreeing, 'We caught him and we beat him but….'

'But he kept coming back…'

'He couldn't keep away…'

Captain Muto points at a spot just in front of where the two men are digging. The captain orders Fujita and me to stand the old Korean man in front of the deepening hole—

The old man just blinking—

His mouth hanging open.

Fujita and I push the Korean towards the spot, his body weaving back and forth like rice jelly. I tell him, 'There's nothing to worry about. Just stand over here while we sort this out…'

But the old Korean man looks at each of us now—

The two *Kempei* officers, the Neighbourhood Association officials, the caretaker, the boiler-man—

Detective Fujita and I—

The dead body laid on the newspapers, the dead body partially covered by the blanket—

'*I am here…*'

Then the Korean glances back at the freshly dug ground, at the hole that the caretaker and the boiler-man are digging, and now he tries to run, but Fujita and I grab him and hold him, his body shaking, his face contorted as he cries out, 'I don't want to be killed! I didn't do anything! Please, I want to live!'

'Shut up, *Yobo*!' says someone—

'But I didn't do anything…'

'So why did you just try to escape, *Yobo*?' asks Captain Muto.

'In Japan, innocent men don't run away.'

'Please don't kill me! Please!'

'You lying *Yobo* bastard!'

'Shut up!' shouts the younger *Kempei* officer now, and he points over to the body beneath the blanket, the body laid out in the dirt and the sun by the corrugated-metal doors to the air-raid shelter, and he asks the old Korean man, 'Did you rape that woman?'

And the old Korean man glances again at the body on the newspapers, the body beneath the blanket—

Bloated and punctured...

'Did you kill that woman?'

He shakes his head—

Flesh and bone...

Captain Muto steps forward. The older *Kempei* officer slaps the Korean's face. 'Answer him, *Yobo!*'

The Korean says nothing.

'This *Yobo* is obviously a criminal,' says Captain Muto. 'This *Yobo* is obviously guilty. There's nothing more to say...'

The old man looks up at us all again: the two *Kempei* officers, the Neighbourhood Association officials, the caretaker, the boiler-man, Detective Fujita and I. The old man shakes his head again—

But now all our eyes are fixed on Captain Muto's sword, the *Kempei* man's bright and shining military sword—

The sword unsheathed and drawn—

The blade raised high—

All our gazes slowly falling to one single spot above the old Korean man's back—

One spot...

'It's time!' shouts the younger *Kempei* officer suddenly—

The caretaker rushing back into his cabin-cum-office, shouting, 'The imperial broadcast! The imperial broadcast!'

Everyone turns to stare at the office, then back again to Captain Muto. The *Kempei* man lowers his sword—

'Bring the *Yobo* over to the radio,' he shouts, and marches off towards the caretaker's cabin himself—

And everyone follows him—

To stand in a semicircle before the open window of the caretaker's cabin-cum-office—

To listen to a radio—
Listen to a voice—
His voice...
A voice hollow, sorrowful and trembling—
'To Our good and loyal subjects...'
The voice of a god on the radio—
'Oh, so bravely, off to Victory / In so far as we have vowed and left our land behind...'
I can hear the strains of that song from a sound-truck again, the strains of 'Roei no Uta' and the voice of a god on the radio—
'After pondering deeply the general trends of the world and the actual conditions in Our Empire today, We have decided to effect a settlement of the present situation by resorting to an extraordinary measure...'
'Who can die without first having shown his true mettle / Each time I hear the bugles of our advancing army...'
The strains of the song, the voice of a god, and the heat of the sun beating down on all our hats and all our heads—
'We have ordered Our Government to communicate to the Governments of the United States, Great Britain, China, and the Soviet Union that Our Empire accepts the provisions of their Joint Declaration...'
'I close my eyes and see wave upon wave of flags cheering us into battle...'
The strains of the song, the voice of a god, the heat of the sun, and the men from the Neighbourhood Association on their knees, heads in their hands, already sobbing—
'To strive for the common prosperity and happiness of all nations as well as the security and well-being of Our subjects is the solemn obligation handed down by Our Imperial Ancestors, and which We hold close to heart. Indeed, We declared war on America and Britain out of Our sincere desire to ensure Japan's self-preservation and the stabilization of East Asia, it being far from Our thought either to infringe upon the sovereignty of other nations or to embark on territorial aggrandizement. But now the war has lasted for nearly four years. Despite the best that has been done by everyone—the gallant fighting of military and naval forces, the diligence and assiduity of Our servants of the State, and the devoted service of Our one hundred

million people, the war situation has developed not necessarily to Japan's advantage, while the general trends of the world have all turned against her interests. Moreover, the enemy has begun to employ a new and most cruel bomb, the power of which to do damage is indeed incalculable, taking the toll of many innocent lives. Should We continue to fight, it would not only result in an ultimate collapse and obliteration of the Japanese nation, but also it would lead to the total extinction of human civilization. Such being the case, how are We to save the millions of Our subjects, or to atone Ourselves before the hallowed spirits of Our Imperial Ancestors? This is the reason why We have ordered the acceptance of the provisions of the Joint Declaration of the Powers...'

'The earth and its flora burn in flames / As we endlessly part the plains...'

The song, the voice, and the heat; men on their knees, heads in hands, sobbing and now howling—

'We cannot but express the deepest sense of regret to Our allied nations of East Asia, who have consistently cooperated with the Empire towards the emancipation of East Asia. The thought of those officers and men as well as others who have fallen in the fields of battle, those who died at their post of duty, or those who met an untimely death and all their bereaved families, pains Our heart night and day. The welfare of the wounded and the war sufferers, and of those who have lost their home and livelihood, is the object of Our profound solicitude. The hardships and sufferings to which Our nation is to be subjected hereafter will certainly be great. We are keenly aware of the inmost feelings of all ye, Our subjects. However, it is according to the dictates of time and fate that We have resolved to pave the way for a grand peace for all generations to come by enduring the unendurable and suffering what is insufferable...'

'Helmets emblazoned with the Rising Sun / And, stroking the mane of our horses...'

The endless song, the endless voice, and the endless heat; men on their knees, howling, now prostrate upon the floor in lamentation, weeping in the dust—

'Having been able to safeguard and maintain the structure of the Imperial State, We are always with ye, Our good and loyal subjects, relying upon your sincerity and integrity. Beware most strictly of any

*outburst of emotion which may engender needless complications, or
any fraternal contention and strife which may create confusion, lead
ye astray, and cause ye to lose the confidence of the world...'*

'Who knows what tomorrow will bring—life?'

The song is ending, the voice ending, the sky darkening now; the
sound of one hundred million weeping, howling, wounded people
borne on a wind across a nation ending—

*'Let the entire nation continue as one family from generation to
generation, ever firm in its faith in the imperishableness of its divine
land, and mindful of its heavy burden of responsibilities, and the long
road before it. Unite your total strength to be devoted to the
construction for the future. Cultivate the ways of rectitude; foster
nobility of spirit; and work with resolution so as ye may enhance the
innate glory of the Imperial State and keep pace with the progress of
the world.'*

'Or death in battle?'

It is over and now there is silence, only silence, silence until the
boiler-man asks, 'Who was that on the radio?'

'The Emperor himself,' says Fujita.

'Really? What was he saying?'

'He was reading an Imperial Rescript,' says Fujita.

'But what was he talking about?' asks the boiler-man, and this
time no one answers him, no one until I say—

'It was to end the war...'

'So we won...?'

Only silence...

'We won...'

'Shut up!' shouts Captain Muto, the older *Kempei* officer—

I turn to look at him, to bow and to apologize—

His lips are still moving but no words are forming, tears rolling
down his cheeks as he brings the blade of his sword up close to his
face now, the thick blade catching the last sunlight—

His eyes, red spots on white...

He stares into the blade—

Bewitched.

Now he turns from the blade and looks into each of our faces,
then down at the old Korean man still in our midst—

'Move!' he shouts at the Korean—

'Back over there, *Yobo*!'

But the old Korean man stands shaking his head—

'Move! Move!' shouts the *Kempei* man again, and begins to shove the old Korean back over towards the hole—

Kicking, prodding him with the sword—

'Face the hole, *Yobo*! Face the hole!'

The Korean with his back to us—

The sword raised high again—

Eyes, red spots on white...

The man begging now—

The last sunlight...

Begging then falling, falling forward with a shudder as a cold chill courses through my own arms and legs—

The sword has come down—

Blood on the blade...

Now a desperate, piercing lament whines up from out of the mouth of the old Korean—

My blood cold...

'What are you doing?' the man cries. 'Why? Why?'

The *Kempei* officer curses the Korean. He kicks the back of his legs and the Korean stumbles forward into the hole—

There is a foot-long gash on the man's right shoulder where he has been cut by the *Kempei* sword, the blood from the wound soaking through his brown civilian work clothes—

'Help me! Please help me! Help me!'

Now he claws wildly at the earth, screaming over and over, again and again, 'I don't want to die!'

'Help me! Help me!'

But Captain Muto has lowered his bloody military sword now. He is staring down at the old Korean in the hole—

Each time the Korean comes crawling back up from the hole, the officer kicks him back down into the dirt—

The blood draining from his body—

Into the dirt and into the hole...

'Help me!' gasps the man—

The *Kempei* captain now turns to the caretaker and the boiler-man and commands, 'Bury him!'

The caretaker and the boiler-man pick up their spades again and begin to heap the dirt back into the hole, over the man, faster and faster, as they bury his cries—

Down in the hole...

Until it is over—

Silence now...

My right hand trembles, my right arm, now both of my legs—

'*Detective Minami! Detective Minami! Detective Minami!*'

I close my eyes. *Eyes that are not my own.* There are scalding tears streaming from these eyes. *Eyes I do not want...*

I wipe the tears away, again and again—

'*Detective Minami! Detective Minami!*'

Finally I open these eyes—

'*Detective Minami!*'

There are flags falling to the ground, but these flags are no flags, these buildings no buildings, these streets no streets—

For this city is no city, this country no country—

I eat acorns. I eat leaves. I eat weeds...

The voice of a god on the radio—

Hollow and sorrowful...

Everything distorted—

Heaven an abyss...

Time disjointed—

Hell our home...

Here, now—

Ten minutes past noon on the fifteenth day of the eighth month of the twentieth year of the reign of the Emperor Showa—

But this hour has no father, this year has no son—

No mother, no daughter, no wife nor lover—

For the hour is zero; the Year Zero—

Tokyo Year Zero.   □

GRANTA

THE BASTARD
OF ISTANBUL
Elif Shafak

Whatever falls from the sky above, thou shall not curse it. That includes the rain.

No matter what might pour down, no matter how heavy the cloudburst or how icy the sleet, you should never utter profanities against whatever the heavens might have in store for us. Everybody knows this. And that includes Zeliha.

Yet, there she was on this first Friday of July, walking on a sidewalk next to hopelessly clogged traffic; rushing to an appointment she was now late for, swearing like a trooper at the broken pavements, at her high heels, at the man walking too closely behind her, at every driver who honked frantically when it was an urban fact that clamour had no effect on unclogging traffic, at the whole Ottoman dynasty for once upon a time conquering the city of Constantinople, and then sticking by its mistake, and yes, at the rain... This damn summer rain.

Rain is an agony here. In other parts of the world, a downpour comes as a boon for nearly everyone and everything—good for the crops, good for the fauna and the flora, good for lovers. Not so in Istanbul. Rain, for us, isn't necessarily about getting wet. It's not about getting dirty even. If anything, it's about getting angry. It's mud and chaos and rage, as if we didn't have enough of each already. And struggle. It's always about struggle. Like kittens thrown into a bucketful of water, all ten million of us put up a futile fight against the drops. It can't be said that we are completely alone in this scuffle, for the streets too are in on it, with their antediluvian names stencilled on tin placards, and the tombstones of so many saints scattered in all directions, the piles of garbage that wait on almost every corner, the hideously huge construction pits soon to be turned into glitzy buildings, and the seagulls... It angers us all when the sky opens and spits on our heads.

But then, as the final drops reach the ground and many more perch unsteadily on the now dustless leaves, at that unprotected moment, when you are not quite sure that it has finally ceased raining, and neither is the rain itself, *on that very interstice* everything becomes serene. For one long minute, the sky seems to apologize for the mess she has left us in. And we, with driblets still in our hair, slush in our cuffs and dreariness in our gaze, stare back at the sky, now a lighter shade of cerulean and clearer than ever. We look up and can't help smiling back. We forgive her; we always do.

At the moment, however, it was still pouring and Zeliha had little, if any, forgiveness in her heart. She did not have an umbrella, for she had promised herself that if she were enough of an imbecile to throw money to yet another street vendor for yet another umbrella, only to forget it as soon as the sun came back, then she deserved to be soaked to the bone. It was too late now anyway. She was already sopping wet. That was the one thing about the rain that likened it to sorrow: you did your best to remain untouched, safe and dry, but if and when you failed, there came a point at which you started seeing the problem less in terms of drops than as an incessant gush, and decided you might as well get drenched.

Rain dripped from her dark curls on to her broad shoulders. Like all the women in the Kazancı family, Zeliha had been born with raven-black, frizzy hair, but unlike the others, she preferred to keep it that way. From time to time her eyes of jade green, normally wide open and filled with fiery intelligence, squinted into two lines of untainted indifference inherent only to three groups of people: the hopelessly naive, the hopelessly withdrawn and the hopelessly full of hope. She being none of these, it was hard to make sense of this indifference, even if it were such a flickering one. One minute it was here, canopying her soul to drugged insensibility, the next minute it was gone, leaving her alone in her body.

Thus she felt on that first Friday of July desensitized as if anaesthetized, a powerfully corrosive mood for someone so zestful. Could this be why she had had absolutely no interest in fighting the city today, or the rain for that matter? While the yo-yo indifference went up and down with a rhythm all its own, the pendulum of her mood swayed between two opposite poles: from frozen to fuming.

As Zeliha rushed by, the street vendors selling umbrellas and raincoats and plastic scarves in glowing colours eyed her in amusement. She managed to ignore their gaze, just as she managed to ignore the gaze of all the men who stared at her body with hunger. The vendors looked disapprovingly at her shiny nose-ring too, as if it were a clue to her deviance from modesty, a sign of her *lustfulness*. She was especially proud of her piercing because she had done it herself. It had hurt, but the piercing was here to stay and so was her style. The harassment of men or the reproach of other women, the impossibility of walking on broken cobblestones or hopping into the ferryboats, and even her mother's constant nagging... There was no power on earth that could prevent Zeliha, who was taller than most women in this city, from donning miniskirts of glaring colours, tight-fitting blouses that displayed her ample breasts, satiny nylon stockings, and yes, those towering high heels.

Now, as she stepped on another loose cobblestone and watched the puddle of sludge underneath splash dark stains on her lavender skirt, Zeliha unleashed another long chain of curses. She was the only woman in the whole family and one of the few among all Turkish women who used foul language so unreservedly, vociferously and knowledgeably; thus, whenever she started swearing, she kept going as if to compensate for all the rest. This time was no different. As she ran, Zeliha swore at the municipal administration, past and present, for never fixing these cobblestones. Before she was done swearing, however, she abruptly paused and lifted her chin, as if suspecting someone had called her name, but rather than looking around for an acquaintance, she instead pouted at the smoky sky. She squinted, sighed a conflicted sigh and then unleashed another profanity, only this time against the rain. Now, according to the unwritten and unbreakable rules of her grandmother Petite-Ma, *that* was sheer blasphemy. You might not like the rain, you certainly did not have to like it, but under no circumstances should you curse at anything that came from the skies, because nothing poured from above on its own. Behind it all there was Allah the Almighty.

Surely Zeliha knew the unwritten and unbreakable rules of Petite-Ma, but on this first Friday of July she felt spoiled enough not to care. Besides, whatever had been uttered had been uttered, just as whatever had been done in life had been done. Zeliha had no time for regrets. She was late for her appointment with the gynaecologist. Not a negligible risk, indeed, given that the moment you notice being late for an appointment with the gynaecologist, you might decide not to go there at all.

A yellow cab with bumper stickers all over its back fender pulled up short. The driver, a rough-looking, swarthy man with a Zapata moustache and a gold front tooth, had all the windows down and a local radio station blasting Madonna's 'Like a Virgin' full bore. He cocked his head out of the window, whistled at Zeliha and barked, 'I'll have some of that!' His next words were muffled by Zeliha's.

The perfect gift.

A gift of *Granta* is perfect for friends and relatives who share your love of reading; there is no risk of sending something that they have already read, and the pleasure will extend all year!

With every order you will receive a free 2007 *Granta* diary worth $14.95, which you can keep for yourself or give with your subscription gift.

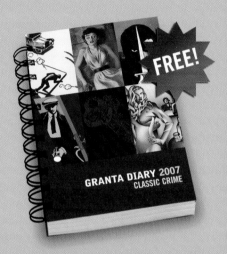

Buy today and you can give four issues of *Granta* and a 2007 *Granta* diary for only $31.25* – that's a saving of over 50% off bookshop prices.

This offer is limited to existing *Granta* subscribers only and diary stock is limited, so reply now to secure your order.

GRANTA

'Top-notch journalism, memoir, fiction, essay, and photography'
Chicago Tribune

* US delivery rate, see overleaf for overseas delivery details

Please complete the form overleaf.

Yes, I'd like to give Granta as a gift.
Please reserve the following subscriptions:

Number of subscriptions	Delivery region	Price per subscription	**Saving**
☐	UK/USA	$31.25	**57%**
☐	Europe/S. America	$40.00	**46%**
☐	Canada & rest of world	$43.25	**42%**

BILLING DETAILS

All prices include delivery!

Title: Initial: Surname:

Address:

Zip:

Telephone: Email:

GIFT ONE DELIVERY DETAILS

Title: Initial: Surname:

Address:

Zip:

Telephone:

Email:

Please start with ☐ this issue ☐ next issue
Please send the free diary to ☐ me ☐ the gift recipient

GIFT TWO DELIVERY DETAILS

Title: Initial: Surname:

Address:

Zip:

Telephone:

Email:

Please start with ☐ this issue ☐ next issue
Please send the free diary to ☐ me ☐ the gift recipient

PAYMENT

[1] I enclose a cheque payable to 'Granta' for $_____ for _____ gift subscriptions to *Granta*

[2] Please debit my ☐ Mastercard ☐ Visa ☐ Amex for $_____ for _____ gift subscriptions

Card number: ☐☐☐☐ ☐☐☐☐ ☐☐☐☐ ☐☐☐☐   96USS

Expiry date: ☐☐ / ☐☐   Signed _____ Date _____

Please return this form to Granta Subscriptions at: PO Box 58, Avenel, NJ 07001

GRANTA

Please tick if you would prefer not to receive occasional offers from compatible companies by post ☐ by phone ☐ by email ☐

'What's wrong with you, creep? Can't a woman walk in peace in this city?'

'But why walk when I could give you a ride?' the driver asked. 'You wouldn't want that sexy body to get wet, would you?'

As Madonna cried in the background *'My fear is fading fast / Been saving it all for you,'* Zeliha began to swear, thus breaking another unwritten and unbreakable rule, this time not one of Petite-Ma's but one of Female Prudence: never cuss at your harasser.

The Golden Rule of Prudence for an Istanbulite Woman: When harassed on the street, never respond, since a woman who responds, let alone swears at her harasser, shall only fire up the enthusiasm of the latter!

Zeliha knew better than to violate this rule, but this first Friday of July was like no other, and there was now another self unleashed in her, more carefree and brash, and frighteningly furious. It was this other Zeliha that took charge of things now, making decisions in the name of both. That must be why she continued to curse at the top of her voice. As she drowned out Madonna, pedestrians and umbrella vendors gathered to see what trouble was brewing. In the turmoil, the man behind her flinched, knowing better than to mess with a madwoman. But the cab driver was neither as prudent nor as timid, for he welcomed all the fuss with a grin. Zeliha noticed how white and flawless the man's teeth were, and could not help wondering if they were porcelain-capped. Little by little, she once again felt that wave of adrenaline escalate in her belly, churning her stomach, accelerating her pulse, making her sense that she might someday kill a man.

Fortunately for Zeliha, the driver of a Toyota behind the cab lost patience and honked. As if awakened from a bad dream, Zeliha came to her senses and shivered at her grim situation. Her proclivity to violence scared her, as it always had. In an instant she veered aside, trying to inch her way through the crowd. Yet in her haste, Zeliha's right heel became stuck under a loose cobblestone. Infuriated, she pulled her foot out of the puddle under the stone. While her foot and shoe came loose, the heel of her shoe broke, thus reminding her of another rule she should never have put out of her mind.

The Silver Rule of Prudence for an Istanbulite Woman: When harassed on the street, do not lose your nerve, since a woman who loses her nerve in the face of harassment and reacts excessively will only make matters worse for herself!

The cab driver laughed, the horn of the Toyota behind blared yet again, the rain hastened on and several pedestrians tsk-tsked in unison, though it was hard to tell what exactly they were reprimanding. Amid all the tumult, Zeliha caught sight of an iridescent bumper sticker glittering on the back of the cab: DON'T CALL ME WRETCHED! As she stood blankly staring at these words, she felt tired beyond herself. Soon the cab and the Toyota left and the pedestrians went their separate ways, leaving Zeliha there, holding the broken heel of her shoe as tenderly and despondently as if she were carrying a dead bird.

Zeliha straightened up and did her awkward best to walk with one heel. Soon she was hurrying amid a crowd with umbrellas, exposing her stunning legs, limping her way like a note out of tune. She was a thread of lavender fallen into a tapestry of browns, greys, and more browns and greys. Though of a discordant colour, the crowd was cavernous enough to swallow her disharmony and bring her back into its cadence. The crowd was not a conglomeration of hundreds of breathing, sweating and aching bodies, but one single breathing, sweating and aching body under the rain. Rain or sun made little difference. Walking in Istanbul meant walking in tandem with the crowd.

As Zeliha passed by dozens of rough-looking fishermen silently standing side by side along the old Galata Bridge, each holding an umbrella in one hand and a spinning rod in the other, she envied them for their capacity for stillness, this ability to wait for hours for fish that did not exist, or if they did, the fish that turned out to be so tiny that they could only be used as bait for other fish that would never get caught. How amazing was this ability to achieve plenty by achieving little, to go home empty-handed yet still satisfied at the end of the day! In this world, serenity generated luck and luck generated felicity, or so Zeliha suspected. It was all she could do, for she had never before tasted that kind of serenity, and she didn't think she ever could. At least not today.

Despite her hurry, Zeliha slowed down as she wound her way through the Grand Bazaar. She had no time for shopping but would go inside for just a quick glance, she assured herself as she surveyed the store fronts. She lit a cigarette and as the smoke curled from her mouth she felt better, almost relaxed. A woman who smoked on the streets was not highly regarded in Istanbul, but who cared? Hadn't she already waged war against the entire society? With that thought she moved towards the older section of the bazaar.

There were vendors here who knew Zeliha on a first-name basis, especially the jewellers. She had a soft spot for glittery accessories. Crystal hairpins, rhinestone brooches, lustrous earrings, pearly boutonnières, zebra-stripe scarves, satin satchels, chiffon shawls, silk pom-poms and shoes, always with high heels. She had never passed this bazaar without ducking into several stores, bargaining with the vendors, and ending up paying far less than the amount proposed for things she had not planned to purchase in the first place. But today she drifted by a few stalls and peeped into some windows. That was it.

Zeliha lingered in front of a stand full of jars, pots and flasks full of herbs and spices. She remembered one of her three sisters asking her this morning to get some cinnamon, though she couldn't remember which one had asked. Zeliha was the youngest of four girls who could not agree on anything but retained an identical conviction of always being right, and a feeling that each had nothing to learn from the others but lots to teach. It felt as bad as missing the lottery by a single number: however you considered the situation, you could not avoid feeling subjected to an injustice beyond correction.

All the same, Zeliha purchased some cinnamon, not the crushed powder, but sticks. The vendor offered her tea and a cigarette and a chat, and she rejected none. While she sat there talking, her eyes nonchalantly scanned the shelves until they locked on to a glass tea set. That too was among the list of the things she could not resist buying: tea glasses with gilded stars and thin, delicate spoons and brittle saucers with gilded belts around their rims. There were already at least thirty different glass tea sets at home, all bought by her. But there was no harm in buying another set, for they broke so easily. 'So damn fragile...' muttered Zeliha under her breath. She was the only one among the Kazancı females capable of getting infuriated at tea glasses when they broke. Seventy-seven-year-old Petite-Ma had a different approach: 'There goes another evil eye!' she exclaimed each time a tea glass broke. 'Did you hear that ominous sound? Crack! Oh, it echoed in my heart! That was somebody's evil eye, so jealous and malicious.'

May Allah protect us all!' But Petite-Ma also heaved a sigh of relief when tea glasses broke. Given that you could not completely wipe out wicked people from the surface of this madly spinning world, it was far better to have their evil eye ram into a frontier of glass than penetrate deep inside God's innocent souls and ruin their lives.

Twenty minutes later, when Zeliha rushed into a chic office in one of the most well-off quarters of the city, she had a broken heel in one hand and a new set of tea glasses in the other. Once inside the door, she was dismayed to remember that she had left the wrapped cinnamon sticks at the Grand Bazaar.

In the waiting room there were three women, each with terrible hair, and a man with almost none. Zeliha instantly noted and cynically deduced from the way they sat that the youngest was the least worried of all; she was languidly leafing through the pictures in a women's magazine, too lazy to read the articles, probably here to renew her prescription for birth control pills. The plump blonde next to the window, who seemed to be in her early thirties and whose black roots begged to be dyed, was swaying on her feet nervously, her mind apparently elsewhere; she was probably here for a routine check-up and annual Pap test. The third one, who was wearing a headscarf and had come along with her husband, seemed to be the least composed, the corners of her mouth turned down, her eyebrows knitted. Zeliha guessed she was having trouble getting pregnant. Now *that*, Zeliha assumed, could be bothersome, depending on one's perspective. She personally did not see infertility as the worst thing that could happen to a woman.

'Hellooo, you!' chirped the receptionist, forcing herself into a goofy, phoney smile so well practised it looked neither goofy nor phoney. 'Are you our three o'clock appointment?'

The receptionist seemed to be having a hard time pronouncing the letter *r* and, as if to compensate for the problem, she went to extraordinary lengths by accentuating the sound, raising her voice, and offering an extra smile whenever her tongue bumped into that ominous letter. To save her the bother, Zeliha nodded instantly and perhaps too heartily.

'And what exactly are you here for, Miss Three-o'clock-Appointment?'

Zeliha managed to ignore the absurdity of the question. By now she knew too well that it was precisely this unconditional and all-embracing female cheerfulness that she sorely lacked. Some women were devoted *smilers*; they smiled with a Spartan sense of duty. How could one ever learn to do so naturally something so unnatural, Zeliha wondered. But leaving aside the question that tugged at the edges of her mind, she responded, 'An abortion.'

The word hovered in the air, and they all waited for it to sink. The receptionist's eyes grew small, then large, while the smile on her face disappeared. Zeliha couldn't help feeling relieved. After all, unconditional and all-embracing female cheerfulness brought out a vindictive streak in her.

'I have an appointment,' Zeliha said, tucking a ringlet behind her ears while letting the rest of her hair fall around her face and over her shoulders like a thick, black burka. She lifted her chin, accentuating her aquiline nose, and felt the need to repeat, a notch louder than she had intended, or maybe not. 'Because I need to have an abortion.'

Torn between impartially registering the new patient and giving a scolding eye, the receptionist stood still, a huge, leather-covered notebook lying open in front of her. A few more seconds passed before she started scribbling. In the meantime Zeliha muttered, 'I'm sorry that I'm late'—the clock on the wall indicated that she was forty-six minutes late and as her gaze rested on it, for a second, she looked as if she were drifting away—'It's because of the rain...'

That was a little unfair to the rain, since the traffic, the broken cobblestones, the municipality, the stalker and the cab driver, not to mention the stop for shopping, should also have been held accountable for her delay. But Zeliha decided to bring up none of those. She might have violated the Golden Rule of Prudence for an Istanbulite Woman, she might also have violated the Silver Rule of Prudence for an Istanbulite Woman, but she held her ground to abide by the Copper Rule.

The Copper Rule of Prudence for an Istanbulite Woman: When harassed on the street, you'd better forget about the incident as soon as you are on your way again, since to recall the incident all day long will only further rack your nerves!

Zeliha knew that if she had brought up the harassment now, the other women, far from being supportive, would have the tendency to pass judgement on a harassed *sister* in cases like these. So she kept her answer short.

'Your age, miss?' the receptionist wanted to know.

Now *that* was an annoying question, and utterly unnecessary. Zeliha squinted at the receptionist as if she were some sort of semi-darkness one needed to adjust one's eyes to see better. All of a sudden, she had remembered the sad truth about herself: her age. Like too many women used to acting above and beyond their years, she was disturbed by the fact that she was far younger than she'd like to be.

'I am,' she conceded, 'nineteen years old.' As soon as the words came out of her mouth, she blushed, as if caught naked in front of all these people.

'We'd need the consent of your husband, of course,' the receptionist continued, no longer in a chirpy voice, and wasted no time in proceeding to another question, the answer of which she already suspected. 'May I ask you, are you married, miss?'

From the corner of her eye Zeliha noticed the plump blonde on her right and the headscarved woman on her left wriggle uncomfortably. As the inquisitive gaze of every person in the room weighed heavier upon her, Zeliha's grimace evolved into a beatific smile. Not that she was enjoying the tortuous moment, but the indifference deep underneath had just whispered to her not to mind other people's opinions since they would make no difference at the end of the day. Lately she had decided to purge certain words from her vocabulary and now that she recalled that decision, why not start with the word *shame*. Still, she didn't have the nerve to utter aloud what by now everyone in the room had fully understood. There was no husband to consent to this abortion.

Fortunately for Zeliha, the fact that there was no husband turned out to be an advantage in formalities. Apparently she didn't need to get anyone's written approval. The bureaucratic regulations were less keen to rescue babies born out of wedlock than those born to married couples. A fatherless baby in Istanbul was just another bastard, and a bastard just another sagging tooth in the city's jaw, ready to fall out at any time.

'Your birthplace?' the receptionist continued drearily.

'Istanbul!'

'Istanbul?'

Zeliha shrugged as if to say, where else could it be? Where else on earth but here? She belonged to this city! Wasn't that visible on her face? After all, Zeliha considered herself a true Istanbulite, and as if to reprimand the receptionist for failing to see such an apparent fact, she turned back on her broken heel and invited herself to the chair next to the headscarved woman. It was only then that she took notice of the latter's husband, who was sitting still, almost paralysed with embarrassment. Rather than passing judgement on Zeliha, the man seemed to be wallowing in the discomfort of being the only male in such a blatantly feminine zone. For a second Zeliha felt sorry for him. It occurred to her to ask the man to step out on to the balcony and have a smoke with her, for she was sure he smoked. But that could be misinterpreted. An unmarried woman could not ask such questions of married men, and a married man would display hostility towards another woman when next to his wife. Why was it difficult to become friends with men? Why did it always have to be like that? Why couldn't you just step out on to the balcony and have a smoke and exchange a few words, and then go your separate ways? Zeliha sat there silently for one long moment, not because she was exhausted, which she was, or because she was fed up with all the attention, which she was as well, but because she wanted to be next to the open window; she was hungry for the sounds of the street. A street vendor's husky voice infiltrated the room: 'Tangerines... Fragrant, fresh tangerines...'

'Good, keep shouting,' Zeliha muttered to herself. She didn't like silence. As a matter of fact, she abhorred silence. It was okay that people stared at her on the street, in the bazaar, in the doctor's waiting room, here and there, day and night; it was all right that they watched and gawked and eyeballed at length again as if seeing her for the first time. One way or another she could always fight against their gaze. What she could not possibly fight against was their silence. 'Tangerinist, tangerinist... How much does a kilo cost?' a woman yelled from an open window on the upper floors of a building across the street. It had always amused Zeliha to see how easily, almost effortlessly, the denizens of this city were capable of inventing unlikely names for ordinary professions. You could add an -ist to almost everything sold in the market, and the next thing you knew, you had yet another name to be included in the list of urban professions. One could easily be called a 'tangerinist', a 'waterist', a 'bagelist'. Or...an 'abortionist'.

By now Zeliha had no doubt. Not that she needed one to know what she already was sure about, but she had also had a test done at the newly opened clinic in their vicinity. On the day of the 'grand opening' the people at the clinic had given a showy reception for a bunch of selected guests, and had lined up all the bouquets and garlands right outside at the entrance so that the passers-by on the street could be informed about the occasion as well. When Zeliha had visited the clinic the next day, most of these flowers had already faded, but the flyers were as colourful as before. FREE PREGNANCY TEST WITH EACH BLOOD SUGAR TEST they said in phosphorescent capital letters. The correlation between the two was unknown to Zeliha, but she had taken the test all the same. When the results arrived her blood sugar turned out to be normal and she turned out to be pregnant.

'Miss, you can come in now!' called the receptionist as she stood in the doorway, fighting another *r*, this time one that was hard to avoid in her profession. 'The doctor…he is waiting for you.'

Grabbing her box of tea glasses and the broken heel, Zeliha jumped to her feet. She felt all the heads in the room turn towards her, recording her every gesture. Normally, she would have walked as rapidly as she could. At the moment, however, her moves were visibly slow, almost languorous. Just when she was about to leave the room, she paused and turned around, knowing exactly whom to look at. There, at the centre of her gaze, was a most embittered face. The headscarved woman grimaced, her brown eyes shadowed by resentment, her lips moving and cursing the doctor and this nineteen-year-old about to abort the child Allah should have bestowed not on a slapdash girl, but on her.

The doctor was a burly man who communicated strength through his erect posture. Unlike his receptionist, there was no judgement in his stare, no unwise questions on his tongue. He seemed to welcome Zeliha in every way. He made her sign some papers, and then more papers in case anything went wrong during or after the procedure. Next to him, Zeliha felt her nerve slacken and her skin thin out, which was too bad because whenever her nerves slackened and her skin thinned out, she became as fragile as a tea glass, and whenever she became as fragile as a tea glass, she couldn't help but come close to tears. And *that* was one thing she truly hated.

Harbouring profound contempt for weepy women ever since she was a little girl, Zeliha had promised herself never to turn into one of those walking miseries who scattered tears and nit-picky complaints everywhere they went. She had forbidden herself to cry. To this day, she had on the whole managed pretty well to stick to her promise. When and if tears welled up in her eyes, she simply held her breath and remembered her promise. So on this first Friday of July she once again did what she had always done to stifle the tears: she took a deep breath and thrust her chin upward as an indication of strength. This time, however, something went wrong and the breath she had held came out as a sob.

The doctor did not look surprised. He was used to it. The women always cried.

'There, there,' he said, trying to console Zeliha while putting on a pair of surgical gloves. 'It's going to be all right, don't you worry. It's only a slumber. You'll sleep, you'll dream, and before you finish your dream, we'll wake you up and you'll go home. After that, you'll remember nothing.' The doctor patted her shoulder, handed her a tissue, and then handed her the whole box. He always had a spare box of tissues ready by his desk. Drug companies distributed these tissue boxes free of charge. Along with pens and notebooks and other things that carried their company name, they made tissues for women patients who could not stop crying.

'Figs... Delicious figs... Good ripe figs!'

Was it the same vendor or a new one? What did his customers call him...? Figist? Zeliha thought to herself, as she laid still on a table in a room unnervingly white and immaculate. Neither the accoutrements nor even the knives scared her as much as this absolute whiteness. There was something in the colour white that resembled silence. Both were emptied of life.

Zeliha grew distracted by a black spot on the ceiling. The more she fixed her stare on it, the more the spot resembled a black spider. First it was still, but then it started to crawl. The spider grew bigger as the injection started to spread in Zeliha's veins. In a few seconds she was so heavy she could not move a finger. As she tried to resist being carried away by the anaesthetized slumber, she started to sob again.

'Are you sure this is what you want? Perhaps you would like to mull it over,' said the doctor in a velvety voice, as if Zeliha was a pile of dust and he was afraid of brushing her away with the wind of his words if he spoke louder. 'If you'd like to reconsider this decision, it is not too late.'

But it was. Zeliha knew it had to be done now, on this first Friday of July. Today or never. 'There is nothing to consider. I cannot have her,' she heard herself blurt out.

The doctor nodded. As if waiting for this gesture, all of a sudden the Friday prayer poured into the room from the nearby mosque. In seconds another mosque joined in and then another and another. Zeliha's face contorted in discomfort. She hated it when a prayer originally designed to be called out in the pureness of the human voice was dehumanized into an electro-voice roaring over the city from microphones and cabinet speakers. Soon the clamour was so deafening she suspected there was something wrong with the loudspeaker system of each and every mosque in the vicinity. Either that or her ears had become extremely sensitive.

'It will be over in a minute. Don't worry.'

It was the doctor speaking. Zeliha looked at him quizzically. Was her contempt for the electro-prayer so obvious on her face? Not that she minded. Among all the Kazancı women she was the only one who was openly irreligious. As a child it used to please her to imagine Allah as her best friend, which was not a bad thing, except that her other best friend was a garrulous, freckled girl who had made smoking a habit at the age of eight. The girl happened to be the daughter of their cleaning lady, a chubby Kurdish woman with a moustache she did not always bother to shave. Back in those days, the cleaning lady used to come to their house twice a week, bringing her daughter along on each visit. Zeliha and the girl became good friends after a while, even cutting their index fingers to mix their blood and become lifelong blood-sisters. For a week the two girls went around with bloody bandages wrapped around their fingers as a sign of their sisterhood. Back in those days whenever Zeliha prayed it would be this bloody bandage she'd be thinking about—if only Allah, too, could become a blood-sister...*her* blood-sister.

Pardon me, she would apologize, and then repeat again and again—because whenever you apologized to Allah you had to do it thrice: *pardon me, pardon me, pardon me.*

It was wrong, she knew. Allah could not and should not be personified. Allah did not have fingers, or blood for that matter. One had to refrain from attributing human qualities to him—that's to say, Him—which was not easy since every one of his—that's to say, His—ninety-nine names happened to be qualities also pertinent to human beings. He could see it all but had no eyes; He could hear it all but had no ears; He could reach out everywhere but had no hands... Out of all this information eight-year-old Zeliha had drawn the conclusion that Allah could resemble us, but we could not resemble Him. Or was it vice versa? Anyway, one had to learn to think about him—that's to say, Him—without thinking of Him as him.

The chances are she would not have minded this as much if one afternoon she had not spotted a bloody bandage around her older sister Feride's index finger. It looked like the Kurdish girl had made her a blood-sister too. Zeliha felt betrayed. Only then it dawned on her that her real objection to Allah was not his—His—not having any blood but rather having too many blood-sisters, too many to care for so as to end up not caring for anyone.

The episode of friendship had not lasted long after that. Since the house was so big and dilapidated and her mother so grumpy and mulish, the cleaning lady quit after a while, taking her daughter away. Having been left without a best friend, Zeliha felt a subtle resentment, but she hadn't quite known towards whom—to the cleaning lady for quitting, to her mother for making her quit, to her best friend for playing two sides, to her older sister for stealing her blood-sister, or to Allah. The others being utterly out of her reach, she chose Allah. Having felt like an infidel at such an early age, she saw no reason why she shouldn't do so as an adult.

Another call to prayer from another mosque joined in. The prayers multiplied in echoes, as if drawing circles within circles. Oddly enough, at this moment in the doctor's office, she worried about being late for dinner. She wondered what would be served at the table this evening, and which one of her three sisters had done the cooking. Each of her sisters was good with a particular recipe, so depending on the cook of the day she could pray for a different dish. She craved stuffed green peppers—a tricky dish to pray for, since every one of her sisters made it so differently. *Stuffed...green...peppers.* Her breathing slowed while the spider started to descend. Still trying to stare at the ceiling,

Zeliha felt as if she and the people in the room were not occupying the same space.

It was too bright here, almost glossy. Slowly and cautiously, she walked along a bridge teeming with cars and pedestrians, and motionless fishermen with worms wiggling at the end of their spinning rods. As she navigated among them, every cobblestone she stepped on turned out to be loose and, to her awe, there was only a void underneath. Soon she'd realize in horror that what was below was also above, and it was raining cobblestones from the blue skies. When a cobblestone fell from the sky, a cobblestone disappeared from the pavement below. Above the sky and under the ground, there was the same thing: a void.

As cobblestones rained from above, enlarging further the cavity underneath, she panicked, afraid of being swallowed by the hungry abyss. 'Stop!' she cried out as the stones kept rolling under her feet. 'Stop!' she commanded the vehicles speeding towards her and then running her over. 'Stop!' she begged the pedestrians shouldering her aside. 'Please stop!'

When Zeliha woke up she was alone, nauseous, and in an unfamiliar room. How on earth she could have walked here was a puzzle she had no desire to solve. She felt nothing, neither pain nor sorrow. So, she concluded, in the end the indifference must have won the race. It wasn't only her baby but her senses too that had been aborted on that pure white table in the next room. Perhaps there was a silver lining somewhere. Perhaps now she could go fishing, and finally manage to stand still for hours on end without feeling frustrated or left behind, as if life was a swift hare she could only watch from a distance but never catch.

'There you are, finally back!' The receptionist was standing by the door, arms akimbo. 'Goodness gracious! What a fright! How you scared us! Do you have any idea how you shrieked? It was so awful!'

Zeliha lay still, without blinking.

'The pedestrians on the street must have thought we were slaughtering you or something... I only wonder why the police did not show up at our door!'

Because it is the Istanbul police you are talking about, not some brawny cop in an American movie, Zeliha thought to herself as she finally allowed herself a blink. Still not quite understanding why she had annoyed the receptionist but seeing no point in annoying her any further, she offered the first excuse that came to her mind: 'Maybe I screamed because it hurt…'

'It could not possibly, miss, for the doctor…has not performed the operation. We have not even laid a hand on you!'

'What do you mean…?' Zeliha faltered, trying less to find out the answer than to comprehend the weight of her own question. 'You mean… You have not—'

'No, we haven't.' The receptionist sighed, holding her head as if at the onset of a migraine. 'There was absolutely no way the doctor could do anything with you screaming at the top of your voice. You did not pass out, woman, no way;. First you were blathering, and then you started yelling and cursing. I've never seen anything like it in fifteen years. It must have taken the morphine twice as long to take effect on you.'

Zeliha suspected some exaggeration behind this statement but did not feel like arguing. Two hours into her visit to the gynaecologist she had come to realize that a patient was expected to talk only when asked to.

'And when you finally blacked out it was hard to believe that you wouldn't start shrieking again. So the doctor said, let's wait till her mind is clear. If she wants to have this abortion for sure, she can still go for it afterwards. We brought you here and let you sleep. And sleep indeed you did!'

'You mean there was no…' The word she had so daringly uttered in front of strangers just this afternoon felt unutterable now. Zeliha touched her belly while her eyes appealed for a consolation the receptionist was the last person on earth to offer. 'So she is still here…'

'Well, you do not know yet if it is a she!' the receptionist said, her voice matter-of-fact.

But Zeliha knew.

Out on the street, despite the gathering darkness, it felt like early morning. The rain had ceased and life looked beautiful, almost manageable. Though the traffic was still a mess and the streets full of sludge, the crisp smell of the after-rain gave the whole city a sacred air. Here and there children stomped in mud puddles, taking delight in committing simple sins. If there ever was a right time to sin, it must have been at this fleeting instant. One of those rare moments when it felt like Allah not only watched over us but also cared for us; one of those moments when He felt close.

It almost felt as if Istanbul had become a blissful metropolis, romantically picturesque, just like Paris, thought Zeliha, though she had never been there. A seagull flew close, crying a coded message she was almost on the verge of deciphering. For half a minute Zeliha believed she was on the edge of a new beginning. 'Why did you not let me do it, Allah?' she heard herself mutter, but as soon as the words came out of her mouth, she apologized in panic to the atheist in herself.

Pardon me, pardon me, pardon me.   □

GRANTA

TRIDENT
James Buchan

James Buchan

One afternoon last summer, just after high tide at the mouth of Loch Long in the west of Scotland, a large black submarine sat on the surface. Among the yachts and pleasure boats and passenger ferries, she looked a rough customer. There were splashes of rust down her fin, and the anti-sonar tiles cemented to the fin and casing were buckled and coming adrift. She looked as if she had been a good long time beneath the sea. She seemed to absorb the estuary light and pay back only a portion of it to those of us around her, like a cloud across the water.

The day was still for western Scotland, but the submarine did not sit well on the loch. Up on the bridge, and above the main entry hatch on the casing, stood men and officers, their white caps visible. Their postures communicated a sort of exhilaration, as though the men were glad to be very near the end of their two- or three-month cruise. Though the objects of attention, they struck no poses as if, being British submariners, their manliness could not be in doubt. (An old submariner I once knew occupied his off-watch time, in those days before DVDs, in embroidery. His mate knitted sweaters in the demanding Scottish double-yarn stitch known as Fair Isle.)

I asked a sailor, dropping kitchen trash in a bin on the ferry's paddle sponson, what sort of submarine she was.

'A bloody big one,' he said.

Big she was, at least twice the 240-foot length of the boat I was on, the old paddle steamer *Waverley*, and perhaps forty feet in the beam. In the soft western light, she looked fierce, rare, and precious like an endangered sea mammal. I tried to imagine what submarine or submarines were beneath us to protect her at this moment of extreme vulnerability, and whether their sonar could distinguish, over the roar and hiss of the Firth of Clyde and the blowing of harbour porpoises, the unique acoustic signature of PS *Waverley*: the churn of her paddle-wheels, the rumble of her sixty-year-old steam engines, and, from the bar and lounge, the sound of 'Danny Boy' and upset furniture.

For many days afterwards, the scale of the submarine filled my imagination like a mountain. As I dawdled like a tourist on the northern Clyde, I came upon the boat at its various tasks: steaming up Loch Long to off-load her nuclear warheads at Coulport, escorted by her entourage of tugs, Royal Marines commandos and Ministry of Defence police in rigid inflatables curvetting about among the eider ducks; or moored the other side of the Rosneath Peninsula at her home port of Faslane behind a floating anti-ship boom.

Leaning on *Waverley*'s rail or eating cold supermarket sandwiches under the dripping spruces, or searching the airwaves for submarine movements, or harassed by police vehicles on the military roads, I felt like a paparazzo spying on some tainted celebrity. I lodged in bed and breakfast houses of truly Scottish gentility, such that the fate of the United Kingdom's nuclear deterrent is forever associated in my mind with Jack Vettriano prints and wicker holders for toilet rolls. I never learned the submarine's name. The Royal Navy, for reasons of operational secrecy, wouldn't tell me. But she was one of four ships in the Vanguard class, each of them by far the most valuable pieces of moveable property in the United Kingdom. According to the Royal Navy, *Vanguard* and her sisters *Victorious*, *Vigilant* and *Vengeance* each displace 16,000 tons of water when dived. The reason for this gigantic scale and for the broad stepped back aft of the fin or conning tower is their armament. Between the fin and the nuclear reactor that propels the boat's steam turbines are sixteen vertical tubes each seven feet in diameter and holding American-designed Trident D5 missiles. These missiles, about three times the size of the slim Polaris missiles they replaced in 1996, were ordered in the last and most perilous phase of the Cold War in the early 1980s and still evoke the apocalyptic military doctrines of that era.

Each three-stage supersonic missile was designed to rise from periscope depth, carry twelve separate nuclear explosive warheads into space and then drop each of them on a separate target, to an accuracy of approximately 120 metres and with one hundred kilotons of explosive force. In this Armageddon of the imagination, a single British submarine at Faslane could obliterate 1,500 Hiroshimas.

Each of the three boats in service—*Victorious* is in refit—has not one but two dedicated crews known as the port and starboard crews, so that while one set is on patrol, the other is on leave or training at seamanship, weapons handling and sonar at the Faslane base. Each crew comprises 140 officers and men, led by a captain and first officer who have survived the notorious British Submarine Command Course, also known as the 'Perisher' course, so that at any one time each boat can call on four men with many millions of pounds of training in him, training that includes outrunning frigates around the

HMS 'Vanguard' nearing the Clyde Submarine Base at Faslane

James Buchan

Isle of Arran or in the Minch. (Women may launch but not serve in Royal Navy submarines.)

This caviar crewing has been successful. Since June 15, 1968, when HMS *Resolution* left the Clyde on her first cruise, I was told there has not been one minute of the day or night in which one of the nuclear missile boats—first of the Resolution class, then of the Vanguard class—has not been on patrol in the Atlantic or the Arctic oceans. At the time I write this, that is exactly 300 missions. Even in the glorious annals of the British submarine service, which has commissioned 708 submarines since 1901 and won fourteen Victoria Crosses, that is not negligible.

With a maximum submerged speed of twenty-five knots, a safe operating depth of at least 800 feet (according to the Royal Navy, but almost certainly quite a bit deeper), and a suite of electronic countermeasures, the boats are designed to be all but undetectable once out in deep water. I was also told that since *Resolution*'s first cruise in 1968 no British missile boat had ever been detected while on patrol. (Even so, the submarines carry a conventional armament with which to defend themselves, including long-range homing torpedoes named Spearfish.)

Now these assertions do not need to be true to deter a state adversary. In the logic of mutual assured destruction, it is enough for that state to suspect that there might be a British boat with a single nuclear-armed ballistic missile within 4,000 nautical miles of his capital city. As it turns out, only unarmed missiles have ever been launched from British submarines and only down the US Air Force Eastern Test Tange range from Cape Canaveral, Florida, most recently on 12 October, 2005 when *Vanguard* tested her firing systems after her refit at Devonport on the British south coast.

Unlike the United States, which has lost two nuclear submarines (USS *Thresher* in 1963 off New England, and USS *Scorpion*, with her nuclear armament south-west of the Azores, in 1968), the British missile boats have suffered no serious accident involving loss of life or, as far as has been reported, serious radiation hazard. Though peace demonstrators have repeatedly trespassed on the bases at Faslane and Coulport, nobody has been shot.

The cost of all this was given in Parliament on July 20, 2006, by the British Defence Secretary, Des Browne. The Trident system, he said, uses up between 5.0 and 5.5 per cent of the defence budget in 2006–7, or about £1.7 billion a year. This bill meets the running costs of the four boats, the 950 officers and crew, the 500 Royal Marine commandos now deployed at Faslane against terrorist attack, the 110-strong marine police unit patrolling the waters against the peace movement, the maintenance of Faslane and Coulport bases and the No. 9 refit dock at Devonport in Plymouth, the fees to the United States Government to make and store on Britain's behalf fifty-eight unarmed Trident missiles at the naval base at King's Bay, Georgia, and the cost of the Atomic Weapons Establishment in the Home Counties to manage and maintain 200 operational warheads. The same money would pay the fees for all the college students in Scotland for a year and the salaries and expenses of all their professors, or the annual maintenance of all Scotland's roads, railways and ferries.

As for the cost of the capital works to build and support the submarines, those are beyond computation. They must comprise the cathedral-like Devonshire Dock Hall erected in the 1980s at Vickers (now BAE Systems) yard in Barrow-in-Furness in Cumbria to construct the boats; the 25,000-ton covered ship-lift, emergency power station and Trident training school at Faslane; the explosives handling jetty and warhead storage caves at Coulport; the seismic protection at the No. 9 nuclear refuelling dry-dock at Devonport; new investment of £350 million at the bomb factories at Aldermaston and Burghfield; and ten or fifteen miles of wire mesh, concertina barbed-tape, look-out towers and military roads. In reality, the Trident project has been by far the most costly industrial enterprise ever attempted in Britain in peacetime, or at least since the building of the Dreadnought-class battleships in the years after 1906. As for taking all these installations down and making both sea and land safe from nuclear contamination, the UK Ministry of Defence believes our heirs will have to find a further £9.73 billion for which, like old misers, we have left not a single penny in contribution.

Britain is now a rich country and certainly a great deal richer than she was on March 11, 1982, when President Reagan wrote to Margaret Thatcher, addressing her as 'Dear Margaret' and offering 'to supply to the United Kingdom Trident II missiles, equipment and supporting services, subject to and in accordance with applicable United States law and procedures'. The military wastes money. That is what it does. It seems Britain can afford, in money at least, both Trident and gruelling and sanguinary wars in Afghanistan and Iraq.

What Trident offered to its enthusiasts was something beyond price, a sort of perfect security. But the Cold War is over, the Trident missiles and their warheads are not actually pointed at Russia or indeed at anything, and Britain's present enemies are individuals who blow themselves up on crowded buses and trains and can't be located through their hydrodynamic wakes or magnetic scars. To maintain the industrial capacity to build advanced submarines and their sonar and weapons becomes more and more difficult as precision manufacturing has declined as a British industry. Even the shore installations built to accommodate the Trident boats at Faslane and Coulport in the 1980s strained British management and industry to the limit, cost twice as much as budgeted, and overran their deadline by two years.

In reality, the Vanguard-class submarine out in Loch Long is as antiquated as the battleships plunging through heavy seas in wartime newsreels; and the Royal Navy is conscientiously carrying out a specialized mission for which the purpose has vanished, like the daily changing of the candles at Windsor Castle even when the old Queen was not at home. An air of mortality has settled over these great vessels and their colossal Scottish shore fortifications. Not halfway into their service lives, the boats have questions to answer: does Britain need them? Or a successor?

To the east of Loch Long ('the lake of the warship' in Scottish Gaelic), on the other side of the Rosneath Peninsula with its sheep farms and neat villages, is an arm of the sea called the Gare Loch (the 'short inlet' in Gaelic). The glacier that formed this sea loch in prehistory left at its tail two spits of sand, and between them a channel, no more than eight hundred feet broad, known after the village on the west side as the Rhu Narrows. The channel has been repeatedly dredged since 1917, most recently to seven fathoms or 13.4 metres to permit the Vanguard-class submarines to pass. To the landlubber, watching warships gliding between the masts of the Royal Northern and Clyde Yacht Club at Rhu, the Narrows seem an extraordinarily perilous passage for a capital ship, particularly one valued in the books of the United Kingdom government at £800 million, and its far more precious officers and crew.

Yet these same Rhu Narrows have also acted as a weir, so that the Gare Loch above the Narrows runs down to thirty-three metres, and might have been designed for submarine operations. It is deep enough for a boat of *Vanguard*'s size, within reach of the open sea and the attractions of Glasgow, and there is only one way in. As Commander F. W. Lipscomb wrote about the Gare Loch in *The British Submarine* in 1954: 'A coracle could easily be spotted coming too near the base from seaward.'

Faslane lies five or six miles north of the Narrows in a deep bay on the east side. A naval base since at least the time of James IV in the early sixteenth century, its rise to importance occurred at the time that steam power was bringing the northern Clyde into fashion as a resort for the merchants and business people of Glasgow and Greenock. What is now the nuclear armaments depot at Coulport was once the neo-Jacobean Coulport House, built by the photographer-botanist John Kibble with a sensational glass house (that was later dismantled and barged down to Glasgow, where it still stands in the city's botanical gardens). Beneath the new military roads are the remains of stone-embanked carriage drives, and everywhere are neat Victorian resorts—Kilcreggan, Cove, Shandon, Rhu, Garelochhead—with their stone mansions and churches in Banker's Gothic.

Just south of the Narrows is the handsome town of Helensburgh, built by an improving landlord in the eighteenth century with that display of Anglo-Scottish Unionism that seems suspect, even frantic, to the modern Scottish eye. As you climb the hill above the Gare Loch, you pass George Street and Hanover Street, Princes Street, Queen Street, King Street, Charlotte Street. Below you is the waterfront of cigarette smokers and old-fashioned Italian restaurants and no-nonsense public houses. Ahead are some of the grandest and most beautiful streets in Britain, each house a castle with its tint of romance in stained-glass porches or pepper-pot towers, and gardens that turn to Edens in the mild Gulf Stream air. The greatest of these houses, or indeed of all houses, perhaps, is The Hill House, designed by C. R. Mackintosh and his wife, Margaret MacDonald, for the Glasgow publisher Walter Blackie in 1902. At the entrance, I have seen tourists miss their step at the glimpse of an almost supernatural domesticity. Thus, the most militarized district in western Europe is also the scene of retirement and improving leisure, as if the United

James Buchan

States had collected its entire nuclear forces in West Hampton, New York, or the French at Deauville.

The Gare Loch's first serious encounter with submarines came on January 29, 1917, when *K13*, one of an ill-fated class of fast steam boats designed to keep up with the fleet, was on trials from the Fairfields Shipbuilders at Govan on the Clyde. Displacing 1,780 tons when submerged (or a tenth of *Vanguard*), and running on the surface at twenty-one knots, she dived with an open ventilator to her oil-fired boilers as if to prove the maxim of the British submariner Max Horton: 'There is no margin for mistakes in submarines; you are either alive or dead.' The captain and forty-eight men escaped after fifty hours in the forward section, but twenty-nine crew and civilians were drowned. The boat was raised six weeks later, and sent back to service as *K22*. The lost stokers, chargemen, shipwrights, boatswains and Fairfields' men are buried in a little cemetery across the road from the base at Faslane. Beside a ruined medieval chapel, the graves are arranged in the shape of a submarine. Below them is the thundering A814 road, then the wire mesh and razor wire and the guarded North Gate of the Clyde Submarine Base.

The modern naval base at Faslane began life in 1940 in response to the defeat of the British Expeditionary Force in France. Fearing that the south coast harbours would come under sustained German attack, the British Admiralty wanted a new port—Military Port No. 1—in the sheltered west and facing the point of the compass from which American help might be expected. It was at Faslane and a US base at Rosneath across the loch that men and material were assembled for the invasions of North Africa and France. Though the Luftwaffe pulverized Clydeside in night raids in the first half of 1941, the Germans never seemed to have found Faslane.

After the war, the base was abandoned and the site leased for a shipbreaking business. The Gare Loch became a graveyard for warships, with pools of fuel oil clogging the beaches at Garelochhead. Britain's last battleship *Vanguard* and the Cunard liner *Aquitania* ended their lives at Faslane and there are photographs of the German battle cruiser *Derfflinger*, scuttled at Scapa Flow in the Orkneys in 1919, being towed into the Gare Loch on an immense floating dock, her propellers in the air. In 1957, submarines were brought back to Faslane when the Third Submarine Squadron and its depot ship were transferred from Rothesay lower down the Firth.

These boats were powered by internal combustion engines that required oxygen to function. They could run on the surface and, at periscope depth, by means of a snorkel or 'snort', but they needed electric battery power to operate when submerged. Much time was spent recharging batteries on the surface when the boat was vulnerable to detection and attack. The US Navy, under the direction of Admiral Hyman Rickover, had since 1948 been exploring the possibility of using steam turbines, as in the ill-fated British K-class boats, but powered not by coal or oil, which require oxygen, but by nuclear fission, which doesn't. A nuclear vessel would not only stay submerged indefinitely, but could also generate enough power to provide clean air and water for the crew. The only limit to the length of a patrol would be the supply of food and the morale of the crew. On January 21, 1954, USS *Nautilus* was launched from the Electric Boat yard in Groton, Connecticut and within three years was exposing limitations in the British diesel-electric boats and anti-submarine aircraft at Nato exercises.

By now, Britain had detonated its own nuclear bombs and had constructed a prototype naval reactor at Dounreay in Caithness on the north coast of Scotland. In 1958, as part of a 'Mutual Agreement for Co-operation on the Uses of Atomic Energy for Mutual Defence Purposes', the United States agreed to save Britain the cost of development and sell her a Westinghouse reactor and its core of uranium fuel. The reactor and other US components—the 'American sector'—were fitted into a Vickers-built bow and the resulting *Dreadnought*, so named because she marked a similar break with the past as the great Edwardian battleships, was launched on the anniversary of Britain's most stirring naval victory (Trafalgar, October 21) in 1960. Beyond the capacity of the south-coast stations, *Dreadnought* arrived at Faslane in April, 1963. By then, President John F. Kennedy and the British Prime Minister, Harold MacMillan, had agreed that the United States would provide Britain with submarine-launched ballistic missiles as well as their launch tubes and targetting systems, and that Britain would allow the US navy to use the Holy Loch as a base for its Polaris submarines.

As in the case of the Trident Sales Agreement of 1980, Britain would make the warheads and the submarines. The first of the four

James Buchan

British missile boats, HMS *Resolution*, was launched from the
Vickers yard at Barrow on September 15, 1966, and fired her first
Polaris missile down the Atlantic Missile Range on February 15,
1968. That Britain could build an effective submarine of wholly new
design, even with an off-the-peg US weapon system, as well as the
jetties and weapons storage to support it and all in just five years
now seems an industrial miracle.

The same could not be said about the works programme to
accommodate the much bigger Trident missile submarines in the
1980s. The largest and most complex work ever undertaken by the
UK Ministry of Defence, the Trident Works comprised 110 different
contracts, including two monsters: a covered ship lift the size of a
sports stadium on the site of the old ship-breaking yard to allow
maintenance of the pressure hulls and sensors; and the 150-feet-high
covered floating jetty at Coulport so that the warheads from
Aldermaston could be attached to the missile bodies while they were
on board the submarines. Under pressure to complete the work in
time for *Vanguard*'s sea-trials in July, 1992, while all the while the
Polaris boats were sailing in and out, the contract both missed the
trials by two years and ran £1 billion over budget.

Still, the work was done. Unlike the old British naval bases in the
south, such as Portsmouth, Gosport and Devonport which reveal
their proud history in ropewalks, gun wharfs, covered slipways and
powder magazines, the Clyde Submarine Base looks like
Guantánamo Bay at a higher latitude, with its mesh and razor-wire,
watchtowers and sodium lighting. From the water, the ship lift,
explosives jetty and weapons-storage bunkers could be the set of a
James Bond film that has inexplicably fallen into the hands of a
committee. With about 7,000 employees, both military and civilian,
it is easily the largest industrial enterprise in Scotland.

In addition to the Vanguard-class boats are three Swiftsure-class
attack submarines and Royal Marine commandos of 'Commachio
Group' to protect them and their weapons; the Northern Diving
Group which clears unexploded ordnance from the Scottish gunnery
ranges, notably at Cape Wrath; and eight mine hunters. Faslane is
also the base for a long-established Nato air-and-sea inshore exercise
now known as Neptune Warrior. The hotels for 2,500 British and
Nato sailors and other civil operations at the base are operated by

a civilian company, Babcock Naval Services, on a ten-year contract valued at £825 million.

Between the ordering of *Vanguard* and her sea trials, the division of Europe ended and with it the Cold War. Unlike the Resolution-class submarines, *Vanguard* sailed on her maiden patrol on 13 December, 1994 without specific target co-ordinates for her nuclear missiles. Presenting to Parliament a Strategic Defence Review in 1998, George Robertson, the first Labour Defence Secretary, revealed that the UK's nuclear arsenal had been reduced to 'less than two hundred operationally available warheads', all of them with the Trident fleet, and no boat would carry more than forty-eight warheads. The order for missile bodies at the US submarine base at King's Bay, Georgia, was reduced to fifty-eight (or six less than the full complement).

Meanwhile, Robertson said, certain missiles would be deployed in a 'sub-strategic' role: that is, that one or more of the missiles in the load would be armed with a warhead of just one or two kilotons of explosive force for use in a limited attack on a military target. In recognition of the reduced threat, he said, the missile submarines would be available for hydrographic work, equipment trials and general exercises. In November 1998, *Vanguard* paid a visit to Gibraltar and a few months later *Victorious* spent five days in the French naval port of Brest. Nuclear sharpshooter, Admiral's steam-yacht, Oceanographer Royal: British ministers seemed at a loss to know what to do with their once dreadful machines and their expert crews.

This political weakness has not been matched by any corresponding strength of the anti-Trident movement. I missed the Trident Ploughshares peace camp at Coulport in the summer and in all my lazy days on the Gare Loch, I did not see a single protestor. Even their forlorn slogans, TRIDENT OUT! or TRIDENT IS TERRORISM, splashed across bridges and garage doors reminded me only of the absence of people. The Faslane Peace Camp, installed in 1982 at Shandon, was deserted when I called. Like the gardens of Helensburgh, it seemed to be reverting to wilderness.

According to a veteran of the Scottish peace movement, the truth is that the campaign against nuclear weapons waxes and wanes with the diplomatic temperature. It was at its strongest in Glasgow in the early 1960s, when the US Polaris boats and their supply ship and floating dock arrived at Holy Loch, and erupted again during the early 1980s in the crisis caused by the deployment of new land-based missiles (Cruise and Pershing-2 ballistic missiles) in England, West Germany and Italy. Today the anti-Trident movement seems as becalmed as the boats themselves and has lost its purchase even on the Scottish Labour Party. Gordon Brown, the leading Scottish politician, Chancellor of the Exchequer and heir apparent to Prime Minister Tony Blair, said on June 21, 2006 that his Britain would be 'strong in defence in fighting terrorism, upholding NATO, supporting our armed forces at home and abroad, and retaining our independent nuclear deterrent.' As so often with military equipment, retaining means replacing with more expensive.

The Trident missile is not yet obsolete. The United States has plans to extend the lives of its own Trident missiles into the 2040s. The British warheads need only to have their decayed radioactive elements regularly replaced. That leaves the submarines, or rather the mortal parts of them, which are the pressure hulls and the nuclear reactor vessels. Those were built with an expected life of about twenty-five years.

There are no reports that the British nuclear missile submarines have been driven to crushing depths or forced into the kind of manoeuvres that are bread-and-butter to hunter-killer nuclear submarines. One former officer said that, in reality, one of the boats is redundant since only three are needed to keep one on station. *Vanguard*, which has been fitted with a new reactor core to see out her service life, could probably serve until 2025, and the other three into the second half of the 2020s.

Still, since *Vanguard* took fourteen years to design, build, equip and test, a decision on a replacement can't be put off too much longer. On July 4, 2005 the then Secretary of State for Defence, John Reid, told the House of Common that 'decisions on any replacement of the United Kingdom's nuclear deterrent are likely to be necessary in the lifetime of the current parliament.' That parliament will end not later than 2010. Gordon Brown has since shown which way he thinks the decision should go.

What complicates the decision is that Britain now possesses just one submarine builder, the great Vickers yard at Barrow now owned by BAE Systems. Like Electric Boat, the division of General Dynamics in Groton, Connecticut, Barrow depends for its existence on orders for nuclear-powered submarines from the government. Its present contract for three Astute-class hunter-killer submarines all but overwhelmed the yard, but the first in the series is due to be delivered (with assistance from Electric Boat) next June and take up station at Faslane in 2009. Unlike diesel-electric submarines, which the United Kingdom abandoned in 2004, nuclear submarines have no foreign markets that might extend a production line and spread the cost per unit. If some 200 submarine designers and technicians are not to be given their cards, and with them a hundred-year British industry, Barrow needs a new order. The future of Trident thus becomes less a matter of pure strategy and more a sort of country dance in which tricky political and industrial steps must be made at precisely the right intervals.

Of the possibilities under discussion, there are two that are unlikely to be realized. The first is that the United Kingdom simply does not replace the Vanguard boats and is content to leave France as the only nuclear power in western Europe. If the Vanguard story has any lesson for a modern government, it is that it is impossible to predict the strategic situation even ten years in the future. As many as thirty-five states in the world are thought to have the capacity (if not the wish) to build a nuclear weapon. In such a world, it is hard to imagine any British government renouncing its nuclear forces.

There seems just as little chance of the government ordering another specialized ballistic missile submarine, which appears in retrospect to have been a particular creation of the Cold War. Its invulnerability may have helped keep the nuclear peace in the northern hemisphere. But it has little power to dissuade terrorists, and even a state adversary would be likely to launch its attack on Britain by way of irregular forces. In any case, a squadron of missile boats that incorporated all the new weapons and sonar technologies would cost from £20 billion to £30 billion: too much to pay.

What might please some constituencies—the Royal Navy, the House of Commons, industry—would be to insert an extra hull section into the Astute-class design aft of the fin, with a smaller but much more versatile battery of launch tubes. These could hold either nuclear ballistic missiles, or conventional ordnance, unmanned underwater vehicles, equipment for special forces, deployable sensors. At the price of blurring the old distinction between nuclear weapons and conventional high explosive, the new boats might allow the government to announce to the world that it had reduced its 'operationally available' stock of warheads still further. The Vanguard class will then pass into that special corner of the public affection reserved for sea-planes and armoured trains and other military dead ends, memorialized in those laborious marine paintings and prints you sometimes see in men's clubs and military messes: *Sunset on the Gare Loch*, HMS Vengeance *turning to port*, or *Good work*, Victorious!

Conversations with ordinary people in Helensburgh and on the water show a people quite inured to the ugly buildings and fences and the warships filling their windowpanes at sun-up or gliding through the trees. These are people of a particular character, who are proud of the maritime and engineering traditions of the Clyde, and without illusions about the good nature of the world. They know that the Ministry of Defence gives and takes away.

That leaves the Scottish Nationalist Party, who are determined to expel nuclear weapons from Scotland. If the party gains power in elections in May, 2007 to the Scottish Parliament in Edinburgh, it will call a referendum to ask the Scots if they want to break the political union with England. Should the Scottish public choose independence, a Scottish Nationalist government in Edinburgh 'will negotiate the safe removal of Trident from Scotland.' In this eventuality, however unlikely as of today, it is hard to imagine the independent Scottish Defence Force having much need for a 25,000-ton ship lift or sixteen warhead-storage bunkers.

What the people of Helensburgh and Rosneath do not want is a nuclear dump. Even if Coulport or Faslane become partly redundant as bases for a British nuclear ballistic missile flotilla, Coulport might yet have a long, long future as a berth for decommissioned nuclear submarines. These will remain a radioactive hazard for hundreds of years. Of the twenty-seven nuclear submarines built in Britain since *Dreadnought*, twelve are sitting in water or dry dock at Devonport and Rosyth on the Forth. In a forlorn group that you almost miss as you drive round Devonport are *Valiant*, *Warspite*, *Courageous*, *Conqueror*, which sunk the Argentine battle-cruiser *General Belgrano* on May 2, 1982 and came into the Gare Loch flying the skull and crossbones, and *Splendid*, which launched cruise missiles during action off Kosovo and in the Persian Gulf. At Rosyth is *Dreadnought* herself, *Churchill,* the four Resolution-class boats, and *Swiftsure.* Neither yard wants any more. The possibility that Loch Long might turn into a sort of radioactive national park does not appeal to this part of Scotland.

Inland of Faslane and Helensburgh is a long valley, known as Glen Fruin, which drains the military exercise area at the head of the Gare Loch not into the sea but into Loch Lomond to the east. On the Ordnance Survey map, it looks the sort of place not many people go to, the sort of place you can walk for a Sunday in the sun and rain and think about nothing in particular.

The road runs north-west from what was once the Cross Keys public house, passes through plantations, and opens up into a broad valley. Following the looping stream, with trout parr splashing in the shallows, you come on neat farm steadings and the ghosts of ancient turf fences and ash and hawthorn hedges. You pass upwards in clouds of meadow pipits. There is nothing to be heard but the faint roar of the military road, with the base workers returning to their houses in Bonhill, and the buzzards mewing above them.

At the head of the valley is Strone farm, and just above it the remains of the old Admiralty Hydro-Ballistic Research Establishment, which operated a tank to investigate the effects of water on the trajectories and impacts of bombs and torpedoes. (There is a photograph of engineers from Dassault at the station in about 1960, looking as French engineers used to look: brilliantine, leather coats, moustaches, brown-tobacco cigarettes.) Now a shabby training camp, it looks the sort of place homesick army recruits are dropped at midnight. Higher up yet is a stone to commemorate a bloody fight between Clan Colquhoun and Clan Gregor on 7 February, 1603. At the top, beside the remains of the old highlandman's road is the rusted but still intact base-plate of an anti-aircraft battery from the Second World War.

The great blue panorama of the Clyde estuary—sea, hills, islands—stretched to the horizon. I sat down in the heather to eat an apple and thought how industrial and military enterprises last just a moment of a moment, but leave long ruins to intrigue a philosophical mind. Squat in the distance lay the square concrete of Hunterston power station, two of its four nuclear reactors shut down. Further up the Firth stood the 700-foot chimney of Inverkip power station—oil fired, too expensive to run, abandoned. Over by Port Glasgow and Greenock a couple of lonely cranes marked the remmants of Clyde shipbuilding on the lower river. Closer to, on my side of the water, a Royal Navy stores ship steamed towards the munitions jetty at Glen Mallen. Finally, just beneath my aching feet, a Vanguard-class submarine was tied up beside the covered ship lift and unloading her torpedoes.

In these various scenes lay the story of the British twentieth century.

□

GRANTA

CONGO
Guy Tillim

Guy Tillim

Successive wars in the Congo, one starting in 1996, the other in 1998, have left the country devastated. After five years of fighting and an estimated 3.5 million dead, most of them civilians, an agreement was reached in 2003 that called for general elections and a new constitution by 2005. In the first round of elections last summer some 3,400 candidates came forward to contest the 500 seats in the House of Assembly, 800 on the ballot in the capital Kinshasa alone. There were thirty-three presidential candidates. The ballot paper was a six-page poster-sized document with pen portraits of all the candidates that made them hard to recognize. The campaign sloganeering and banners didn't say 'Vote Adam Bombole, Health for All', for example, but 'Vote Adam Bombole, page 4 No. 352'.

Etienne Tshisekedi, leader of the Union for Democracy and Social Progress (UDPS) and a veteran former minister under Mobutu Sese Seko, had called for a boycott of the elections in July. Young men in Kinshasa fought battles with police in his name as they tore down and burned election paraphernalia, directing special hostility at the face of President Joseph Kabila, who succeeded his father, Laurent, after he was assassinated by a bodyguard in 2001. Joseph Kabila was running as an independent, though he was listed as an 'initiator' of the People's Party for Reconstruction and Democracy, which chose him as their candidate.

I asked a Congolese friend if he had a theory about the large number of candidates. 'Visibility is everything,' he told me. 'Get yourself on a list, so when the next thing happens, perhaps a peace agreement where power and influence are divided up, you will be on it somewhere.' Kabila and his main rival, Jean-Pierre Bemba, who have been at war with each other and control separate armies barracked in Kinshasa, have unofficially divided up these spoils for years.

Bemba, who is the leader of the Movement for the Liberation of Congo, a rebel group turned political party, took twenty per cent of the 17 million votes to Kabila's forty-four per cent in the first round. The Kinshasa streets mirrored the wasteland that has been wrought by war between these two men: the lack of basic services, the populist politicking, the violent rallies. But there is a hope that the 450 million dollars, given mostly by the European Union towards the election, will transform this rivalry into a constitutional debate.

Guy Tillim

A statue of Patrice Lumumba erected by Laurent Kabila,
and an unfinished tower built during the Mobutu years look down on
Jean-Pierre Bemba's supporters, Kinshasa, July 2006

Kinshasa suburbs, July 2006

Outside a Lumumbiste Party supporters' office

Overleaf, anti-election protestors attack Kabila's image

Riot police disperse supporters of Etienne Tshisekedi, Kinshasa

Lumumbiste Party supporters pinning up pictures of their leader Antoine Gizenga, who was a deputy to Patrice Lumumba in 1962

This page and overleaf: supporters of Jean-Pierre Bemba line the route as he walks from the airport to a rally in Kinshasa

Overleaf: presidential candidate Jean-Pierre Bemba (centre) at an election rally in Kinshasa, surrounded by his bodyguards

European peace-keeping troops on duty during the elections, Kinshasa, 2006

GRANTA

THE LITTLE MUSEUM OF MEMORY

Mark Slouka

America was my foreground, familiar and known: the crowds, the voices, Captain Kangaroo and Mr Magoo, the great, west-bound trains that clattered and tilted past the crossing as my father and I sat waiting in the car on Orchard Road. Behind it, though, for as long as I can remember, was the Old World, its shape and feel and smell, like the pattern of wallpaper coming through the paint.

My father loved America, loved the West—the idea of it, the grandness and the absurdity of it. It was a vicarious sort of thing. To my knowledge, for example, he never watched a baseball game in his life, yet the knowledge that millions of men cared passionately for it, that they had memorized names and batting averages, somehow gave him pleasure. The time we drove west, my mother in her sunglasses and deep-blue scarf looking like Audrey Hepburn in *Breakfast at Tiffany's*, he was nearly stunned into speechlessness by the vastness of it all: the sheer immensity of the sky, the buzz of a bluebottle under that huge lid of sun, the oceanic valleys stretching to the horizon. The little two-lanes and the sleepy motels thrilled him; every menu was an adventure, and he'd study the gravy-stained paper through his reading glasses as if it were a letter from some distant land, which I suppose it was.

I have a memory of him standing in the open door of some little motel room in New Mexico, leaning against the door frame, smoking. Swallows or bats are dipping under the telephone wires. It's dusk, and the land on the other side of the road opens into endless space—blueing, lunar. It's as if the room, the motel, the gas station down the way could tip into it at any moment and snake like a necklace into a well. My mother's lying on the bed under the light, her legs crossed at the ankle, reading a magazine.

'My God, Ivana, you should come and see this,' my father says. 'I could fit half of Czechoslovakia into the space between the road and those cliffs out there.'

'I'm sure you could,' said my mother.

The West, my father liked to say, especially after he'd had a glass or two of wine in the evenings when we had friends over, back home in New York, was the great solvent of history. It dissolved the pain, retained the shell: 'Paris, Texas; Rome, Arkansas... Just try and imagine it the other way around,' he'd say. 'Chicago, Italy? Dallas, Austria? Unthinkable.' No, the funnel was securely in place. Everything was running one way. Eventually all of Europe, all the popes and plagues, the whole bloody carnival, would be a diner somewhere off the highway in Oklahoma.

'Here he goes,' someone would say.

'Think of it,' my father would say. 'The Little Museum of Memory. The Heaven of Exiles. Entertainment for the whole family.'

When I think back on that close little apartment with the Kubilius sketches in the hallway and the bust of Masaryk by the door and the plastic slipcovers on the new sofa, it seems to me that even when the living room was full of people eating *merunkove kolace* and drinking they were somewhere else as well. I don't quite know how to put it. They seemed to be listening to something...that had already passed. And because I loved them I grew to love this thing, this way of being, and listened with them.

As a child my bed was pushed against the wall to the living room, blocking off a door. A matter of space. My father unscrewed the doorknob and covered the hole with a brass plate and then, because the frame of the door looked so ugly rising up behind my bed, my mother hung a kind of bamboo mat over it to hide it. It was this makeshift curtain, which smelled like new-mown grass, that I would move aside so that I could spy on them as they talked: the Jakubecs and the Stepaneks, Mr Chalupa and Mr Hanus with his two canes... It's odd for me to think, simply by counting up the years that had passed, that they must be gone. Only pieces of them remain: a genteel, slightly tremulous voice, white fingers tightening a bow tie, a musty, reassuring smell, like cloth and wool and shoe polish, which reminded me, even then, of the thrift shops on Lexington Avenue... How quietly, like unassuming guests, they slipped from the world. How easily the world releases us.

Mr Stepanek was a small man who always sat very straight on our couch, as though hiding something behind his back; he had a lot of opinions about things and got into arguments with people because he thought a lot of things were funny. His laugh was like a little mechanism in his throat: a dry, rapid-fire cackle—ha ha ha ha ha ha ha—that always went on a second or two too long. He and my father had been childhood friends—they had grown up in adjoining buildings in the Zidenice district of Brno—and perhaps for this reason he irritated my father in that close, familiar way that only old friends can irritate one another.

I loved Mr Hanus best, but it's Mr Chalupa I remember most clearly, I'm not sure why. He never brought me things. Or talked to me much. Or came into my room and sat on the edge of my bed, as Mr Hanus did, and looked at the pictures on my wall. It was never 'Uncle Pepa is here, look what he brought you,' just 'Say hello to Mr Chalupa, where are your manners?' and I never minded much because I couldn't imagine him any other way. He wasn't interested in me. He'd show up at our door every Friday, carrying his violin case and a bottle of wine in a kind of wicker net and a white paper bag with a loaf of the Irish soda bread my father liked, and say, 'Here, take them, take them,' as though they were an itchy garment he couldn't wait to shed, and my parents would smile for some reason and take the things from him and my mother would say, 'Say hello to Mr Chalupa, what's the matter with you?' and he'd say, 'How are the Beatles, young man? How are the fab four, eh?'—in English, as though he didn't know I spoke Czech—then sink into my father's chair, which used to be by the long white bookshelf in the living room, and tell my parents about the troubles he'd had on the F train in from Manhattan. And that would be it for me.

I remember him well dressed in a suit and tie, a slim man of average height who wore a hat and who always seemed just slightly put upon, as though the world were a vast, wilfully cluttered room he had to negotiate—and quickly—because the phone was ringing on the other side. When I dreamed of him, nearly forty years later, he was sitting in my father's chair on a wide African beach at nightfall, still dressed in his suit and tie. A huge, still lake, backed by mountains, lay before us; behind us, white dunes of shells rose to a distant ridge on which I could see rows of fires and the silhouettes of men and monkeys. He was sitting there with that look on his face, staring irritably at the sand in front of him, ignoring me. I was just about to say something to him when a tall wooden ship, far out on the water, spontaneously burst into flame. He seemed unsurprised. He looked up at the thing—at the blazing masts, the spar like a burning sword, the beating wings of the sails—and, shaking his head slightly, turned his hands palm up without raising his wrists from the armrests, then let them fall back as if to say, 'Well, that's just fine.'

I would spend hours spying on my parents and their friends through the blocked-off door behind my bed. I found that by turning off the light and pushing over the curtain a little, I could see nearly half the living room through the crack between the door and the frame. When Mr Chalupa was there, my father would always sit on the sofa directly below me. Kneeling on my bed in the dark, barely breathing, I'd look directly over the smooth sloping shore of his balding pate to the white bookshelf on the far side of the room. Mr Chalupa sat to the right, his violin and his bow laid neatly across his lap or leaning against the bookshelf. My mother, whom I could see only half of unless she leaned forward to get something from the glass table, usually sat next to my Aunt Luba, who wasn't really my aunt, on the small sofa with the hole below the left cushion in which I used to hide Sugar Daddies before I was discovered.

There was nothing much to see, really. They'd talk and laugh and drink and then, inevitably, the guitars would come out of their cases and the violin bows would be rosined up and the men would take off their jackets and loosen their ties and Mr Chalupa, who played the violin better than anyone else and knew every lyric to every song, would roll up his sleeves and the singing would begin: 'Pri Dunaji Saaty Prala' and 'Mikulecke Pole' and 'Polka Modrych Oci'—Slovak and Moravian folk songs—and eventually, when enough wine had disappeared, dance tunes like 'Na Prstoch si Pocitam' and 'Pitala Mamicka' and 'Ked sa do Neba Divam' and 'Este Raz u tebe Pridem' and on and on till two or three, and sometimes I'd wake up deep in the night and hear them leaving, saying something about their coats or bumping into things by the door, sshhhing each other and laughing. And it seemed to me in those moments that their voices were all that was left of them, that they were good-natured spirits the hours had made insubstantial, and lying in bed I'd listen to them gathering their things, whispering, joking, joining in part of a refrain until, stepping through our apartment door, they disappeared as abruptly as the voices at the end of a record.

Mr Chalupa had escaped from Czechoslovakia in 1948, like most of them, then spent some years in Salzburg, some more in Toronto, another in Chicago, before coming to a temporary rest in our apartment in Queens. The year was 1956. I was six years old. We put him up for a few weeks, during which time he slept in my room and hung his pants over the back of my chair while I slept on a mat on my parents' floor. When he found a place somewhere on the Upper East Side of Manhattan, I moved back into my room. For the next year and a half he continued to come by our apartment every week or two to play his violin.

I saw him for the last time (though I didn't know then that it would be the last time) on a night in January 1958, when he knocked a bottle of red wine against the corner of a shoe rack while taking off his coat in our hallway. It was one of those huge bottles, my father said later, that looked like it had been bought from a Spanish peasant for a cheese or a length of rope, and it soaked everything. Chalupa looked at the mess he'd made—at the small red lake at his feet, at the wine spattered knee-high up the wall, at the neck of the bottle still in his hand—and shook his head. Everything breaks, he said.

No word of concern, no apology. My mother picked up the ruined rug and hung it over the outside railing, where it rained wine into the leafless hedges fifteen floors below, and eventually others came by with more wine and everyone forgot about it. The group spent the evening singing like always, and late that night, when they were all leaving (Chalupa was the last to go), my father said something about seeing him in two weeks and Chalupa said he wasn't sure, and when my father asked why he shook his head as though he had heard that the F train would be out of service on that day and said, 'Melanoma, old man.'

'I saw him once or twice more in the hospital,' my father said, 'but that was that. Between the toes, Antonin. That's where they found it. Absurd.'

I didn't hear the story for a long time, and when I did, it came as something of a shock to learn that Mr Chalupa had been dead for nearly ten years. I had always assumed for some reason that he had simply left New York; that he had been playing in some other circle all those years—picking at someone else's *babovka*. I could see him there, in that other apartment, leaning back stiffly in someone else's reading chair or drumming his small white fingers on the neck of his violin while waiting for the others to return from the kitchen.

For a while, the knowledge that he had died so long ago troubled this picture I had of him, like wind on water. But then the picture re-formed itself, and though I knew it was a lie, it still felt truer than the one which had replaced it. It was as though the fact of his death had left a space—like the chalk outline of a body—in the shape of the thing that had gone. The easiest thing was to bring back the body. It fitted best. There he was again, back in that other apartment in Baltimore or Chicago, playing his violin.

It was not until I moved to Prague that I learned that Mr Chalupa, who had once slept in my room, had also worked for the Gestapo.

I had arranged to meet an old couple I was working with at the time in an outdoor cafe on Londynska Street in the Vinohrady district of Prague. At the last moment the wife couldn't make it, and so it was just me and the old man. It was late May and the cobbles were wet from the rain and the branches dripped water on the umbrellas over the metal tables. Except for a young couple with a miserable-looking dog, we were the only ones there.

We talked for a while about the translation project we were collaborating on, and then the conversation turned to what it had been like growing up in New York in the Czech exile community, and Chalupa's name came up.

'Milos Chalupa?' the old man asked.

'You knew him?'

'Everyone knew him,' he said. 'Or of him. He was some kind of accountant before the war, though I'm not sure what he accounted for, or to whom. During the war he was an interpreter for the Gestapo.'

At that point the waitress, who had been staying inside because of the rain, came out with a rag to wipe the tables that weren't covered with umbrellas. '*Date si dalsi, panove?*' she called to us from across the small patio. Would we like another? '*Ale dame,*' the old man said. A low rumble sounded in the quiet street. It seemed to come from over towards the train yards to the south.

'You're saying Chalupa was a collaborator?' I said.

'Who knows?' the old man said. 'They say he was approached by the Resistance some time in 1941, around the time the RAF dropped those paratroopers who were to assassinate Heydrich into the protectorate. He told them he couldn't help them.'

'So he was a collaborator,' I said.

'Listen,' the old man said, 'if only the heroes were left in Prague after '45—or in Warsaw or Leningrad for that matter—there would be fifty people left between here and Moscow.'

The waitress placed two glasses of wine in front of us and went back inside the cafe.

'Maybe he did it to keep himself above suspicion,' the old man said. 'So that they would trust the picture he gave them.'

'You believe that?' I said.

'I believe it's going to rain,' the old man said, as the first fat drops began to smack down on the cloth above our heads. He leaned over the table to light a cigarette, then dropped the match into a glass on the table next to ours. 'I saw Heydrich once, you know. I was waiting for the tram in front of the National Theatre. They stopped everything, cleared the street. I saw him get out of the limousine. Very tall. I remember he moved his head like this, like a bird.'

'What happened?' I asked him.

'Nothing happened. He walked into the theatre. I walked home.'

It was raining hard now. Everything around us had turned grey. The old man was quiet for a while; I saw his head shake very slightly, as if he were disagreeing with something, though it might have been simply a tremor. He ran his fingers over the back of his hand. 'You see, it wasn't always easy,' he said. 'To tell. To know who was who. Now, take the boys who assassinated Heydrich in '42. A heroic act, a just act, and eight thousand people died because of it. Entire towns were erased from the map.' He shook his head. 'Don't fool yourself; I suspect your parents knew who Chalupa was. We had all heard the stories about him. In the end we just had to choose which one to believe.'

He was quiet for a while. 'Are you dry over there?' he said at last.

'I'm fine,' I said.

'Here's an ugly story for you,' he said.

He couldn't tell me what Chalupa thought, he said, or what he believed. He could only tell me what he had done, which was really all that anyone could say about anyone. There were some facts: after the uprising in 1945 Chalupa hadn't been shot as a collaborator. He'd been at such and such a place at such and such a time. 'X' number of witnesses had confirmed that this or that had been said. It all amounted to little or nothing. The interrogation had focused on a single, well-known event—I could read the report if I wanted. Obviously his questioners had given him the benefit of the doubt, because he'd lived to play the violin in my parents' apartment in New York.

The basic story, he said, began and ended with a woman named Moravcova who lived up in the Zizkov district with her husband and their sixteen-year-old son, Ota. 'You'd have had to see her,' he said. 'A real *Hausfrau* to look at her—thick legs, meaty face, all bosom and bum—she was one of the most important figures in the Prague underground during the war—the anchor. No one did more, or took more chances. Nothing got past her. Nothing. When one of the paratroopers sent from London approached her for shelter in the fall of '41 she supposedly brushed him off at first—even threatened to turn him in to the authorities, and so convincingly that for a few hours he thought he had approached the wrong person—simply because there was something about him that had made her suspicious. London had to confirm, and a second code had to be arranged, before she would take him in. Couldn't risk endangering her boys, she said. And they were all her boys: the paratroopers— two of whom stayed in her apartment posing as relatives looking for work—their contacts...

'She washed and ironed their clothes, went shopping for them. Basically, she did everything. She'd bring parcels of blankets and clothing and cigarettes to the safe houses, travelling by tram, holding them right there on her lap, right under their Aryan noses—not once or twice, you understand, but dozens of times—knowing all the while that if any one of them demanded that she open the package she'd never have time to get to the cyanide ampoule she carried like a locket around her neck. On certain days she would go to the Olsany graveyard to receive and send messages, lighting a candle or pruning back the ivy on her mother's grave, maybe exchanging a few words with someone who might pause at the adjoining plot or tip his hat to her on the path. She was rational, smart, tough as an anvil. What made her special, though, was that she was apparently terrified the entire time. Rumour had it that she took to wearing a diaper, as if she were incontinent, for the inevitable accidents. That after Heydrich was assassinated, when everything was going to hell, she'd pretend to be nursing a toothache and travel with the ampoule already in her mouth, which, if true, was simply madness. The point is that she knew what she was risking, and she risked it anyway.'

The rain had begun dribbling between the two umbrellas I had crossed over our heads and the old man moved his wine out of the way.

'In any case, after Heydrich was hit—it happened right up here, in Liben, though it looks quite different now—things happened very quickly. They carried him out across Charles Bridge at night, torches and dogs everywhere, and before they got him to the other side SS and NSKK units were sweeping through the city, searching neighbourhood by neighbourhood, block by block. Combing for lice, they called it. They were very good at it—very thorough. Wehrmacht battalions would seal off an area, five or six city blocks, and then they'd go apartment to apartment. It's all television now, really. I barely believe it myself. I'll give you an example. Right after Heydrich died, Wenceslas Square was filled with half a million Czechs swearing their loyalty to the Reich. People were hysterical; they knew what was coming. I saw this with my own eyes, and I still don't believe it.

'Anyway, after Heydrich's death, the underground freezes. Moravcova somehow manages to get her family out of Prague. The boy goes to the country; the husband to stay with an army friend in Kralovo Pole. Moravcova herself hides in Brno, which is hardly better. After a few weeks, when nothing happens, all three return one by one to their apartment in Zizkov, who knows why. Maybe they're worried that their absence will be noticed. Maybe they just want to come home.

'Which is where Chalupa, the translator, comes into it. He gets a telephone call at four-thirty in the morning; is told to be ready in five minutes. He doesn't know that the paratroopers hiding in the crypt of the church on Resslova have been betrayed, that they will die in that crypt early the next morning, June 18—that the whole thing in fact has begun to crumble. He just knows that something is wrong.

'You have to picture it. Three cars are waiting in the dark. A door opens, he climbs inside. He has no idea where they're going until he hears the name. Some woman named Moravcova. An apartment in Zizkov. He just sits there on the leather seat, holding his hat on his lap like a truant. What else can he do? No one speaks to him—they don't trust him, naturally, and his ability to speak German only makes things worse because it means he's neither one thing nor the other, hammer or nail.

'It's a quick trip. The city is almost deserted at that hour, and the limousine races through the intersections, crosses Bulhar Circle, then turns left up that long hill there. He knows they'll be there in three minutes, then two, and then they're there and Fleischer—the commanding bastard that morning—is already pounding on the door, swearing, when it opens and a bent, tiny woman appears like a hedgehog in a fairy tale. '*Schnell, wo wohnen die Moraveks?*' Fleischer yells as they shove past her, and Chalupa begins translating when the hedgehog calls out at the top of her lungs, as though she's suddenly been struck deaf, 'Would you like to take the stairs or the elevator, *mein Herr?*' but they don't notice because they're already rushing up the stairs and it's too late for anything at all.

'By the time Chalupa gets there they're all three standing with their faces against the wall, the father and the boy still in their pyjamas, Madame Moravcova in a housecoat, as though she'd been awake all night. *Wo sind Sie, wo sind Sie?*— Where are they?—Fleischer is roaring as the rest of them pour into the other rooms, as the sofa and chairs are pulled from the walls and tipped on their sides, and Chalupa begins to translate: *Kdo, ja nevim...*'—*Wer? Ich weiss nicht...* and then stops because Fleischer has her by the throat and is striking her face, hard and fast, back and forth: *Wo—sind—Sie, Wo—sind—Sie, Wo—sind—Sie?* She sinks to the floor. *Steh auf!* She stands. Please, she says, I have to go to the bathroom, please.

'Chalupa looks at her husband and son. They are both barefoot. There is the smell of shit in the room. The husband's hair is standing up; his right leg is trembling as if he were listening to a very fast song. The boy is looking into the wallpaper. In the transcripts, Chalupa claimed he never saw such terror in a face in his life. Please, I have to go...Moravcova says again. She doesn't look at her husband or her son. Chalupa translates: '*Sie sagt, dass sie zum Klo mus*—She says she must go to the bathroom... And suddenly he understands. Fleischer is striding into the other room, still looking for the paratroopers. *Nein.*

'So there you have the basic situation. A wrecked room. Three people lined up against a wall. A single guard. 'Please, I have to go,' Madame Moravcova is pleading, over and over again. 'Please.' Perhaps she realizes that their lives are over, that life is simply done. Perhaps not. Suddenly someone is yelling from the hallway outside—Stop! Stop!—*Zastavte! Zastavte!*—though maybe it's just *Vaclave! Vaclave!*— the name. Who can tell? They sound alike; anyone could confuse them.

And Chalupa—here's the thing—supposedly translates the first and the bastards run out, thinking the paratroopers have been flushed into the open, and in the five or six seconds before the guard remembers himself and rushes back in, Moravcova sees her chance and takes it, and by the time they push past her fallen body blocking the bathroom door from inside it's too late for the water they pour down her throat to do them any good. So...*Zastavte* or *Vaclave*—take your pick.

'She left her family?' I said.

'Indeed.'

'She must have known what she was leaving them to.'

'I doubt she imagined the particulars. Supposedly they broke the boy the next day when they showed him his mother's head in a fish tank.'

'Good God.'

'Doubtful,' the old man said. 'But we should get to work.'

I remembered Mr Chalupa. He'd slept in my room. I could see that irritated look, the way he would lift his violin out of its case with three fingers, the way he would sink into my father's chair. 'How are the Beatles, young man?' I could hear him say. 'How are the fab four, eh?' □

ReadySteadyBook
a literary site

ReadySteadyBook.com is an independent book review website devoted to discussing and reviewing the very best books in literary fiction, poetry, history and philosophy

Award-winnning Irish poet Dennis O'Driscoll recently described ReadySteadyBook as "unfailingly resourceful and informative ... day after lively day"

"The UK's largest independent literary website"
— The Observer

"A treasure ... with smart, serious analysis"
— The Guardian

www.ReadySteadyBook.com

GRANTA

THANK GOD
WE'VE GOT A NAVY
Brian Thompson

National Service recruits, 1953

Today it is usual—especially among those who have never faced conscription—to describe national service as time wasted, even an offence against civil liberties in some sinister way.

'One thing is certain,' bristling young ideologues have explained to me, as if to some balding warmonger with blood on his hands. 'You would never get our generation to take part. We have come a long way since then. We know far more.'

It is the last sentence that always stops me in my tracks. My conscription notice arrived in 1953, in the middle of the only peace-time period in which England has required national service. For me, it meant a blizzard of people and ideas that I never knew existed. The gates of a very small purgatory opened, casting light on to cheerful chaos, shot through with insanity and heroism in about equal measure.

I spent the first night burning the pimples out of ammunition boots with the back of a spoon heated over a candle; and writing to a girl called Alma, whose illiterate husband, Tony, had yesterday been cleaning vats at Mann's Brewery.

'What do you want me to say?' I asked, holding his warm sixpence in the palm of my hand.

'It ain't difficult. Just that I'm here and all that.'

So saying, he set off with his mates for a cup of tea.

Kempston Barracks, Bedford, was the home of the Beds and Herts, whose regimental history had been given to us earlier in the day by the adjutant. To hear his remarks we had been herded into the chapel, which even to my untutored eye had an air of disuse about it. This being the army, there was due deference to the outward forms expected of a place of worship: the pews glistened and the brass lectern shone. While nobody much cared about the word of God in the ranks of the Beds and Herts, if He ever wanted to utter it in a local setting He would find the place buffed to a nicety.

It was a mild September afternoon and bars of sunlight fell in military precision. Some of the recruits slept, their newly shorn skulls dropping to their chests. The adjutant concluded his historical sketch by dabbing at his lips with a crisply folded handkerchief. When he invited questions, a hand shot up.

'Yes?'

'When do we get our first leave, mate?'

There was a skittering of hobnails on the marble floor as a sergeant plucked this unfortunate questioner from his pew and frogmarched him outside. When we filed out ourselves a few moments later, he was doubling round the parade ground with an empty dustbin raised above his head.

'Everything's fine. I have already made some good mates. A lot of us are from north London, but some are from the country areas. The barracks are not all that old but made to look that way, like a fort in an Alexander Korda movie.'

I considered this last touch, wondering how many Korda movies Alma had seen in her short life. She might be much more interested in Private Wood, who had not stopped crying since his arrival, or Private Tasker, a man-mountain for whom the stores could not supply a uniform big enough. Tasker sat opposite me while I wrote, scratching his shins absent-mindedly, undressed to his drawers, the one item of army clothing sized to fit all. What Tasker called his crown jewels dangled free, not—or not only—because they were in scale with the rest of him, but rather because the drawers themselves were such sorry sketches of male underwear.

'Tell her how much he misses her,' he suggested. 'And chuck in his best regards to the mother-in-law.'

'She might be dead.'

'They never are,' Tasker muttered. 'Don't you have a girl of your own to write to?'

'Yes. How about you?'

'Promised someone a line from time to time. But what can you say about all this?'

Just then the lance corporal in charge of our barrack room approached.

'Put some clothes on,' he said to Tasker. 'This isn't a nancy-boy parlour.'

Lance Corporal Denison was lately a squaddie just like ourselves. He had his own little room and, earlier in the evening, had sauntered out to show us how to improve our trousers by applying wet soap to the interior of the crease before ironing. Explaining how to bone boots, he showed us his own, cradled in his arms as lovingly as twins. The problem with Denison was that he wore glasses, was quite short, and had almost certainly been the butt of the playground bully in a previous existence. Only a little power over others had gone to his head now.

Tasker stood, towering over him, all ivory skin and ginger fuzz. 'Fuck off, sonny,' he said.

Denison was about to put him on a fizzer when someone ran in from the ablution blocks, the wooden 'spiders' where those who needed to shave in the morning could do so in icy-cold water. Private Wood had stopped crying long enough to drink a tin of liquid Brasso. He was spewing his ring and looked a funny colour, this messenger explained. Purple, in fact.

We were all eighteen but that was the only thing we had in common. The letter I had written to Alma was no more than the truth: we came from different backgrounds and had seen very different things. The days when the regiment had been raised from amiable giants like Tasker had long gone. Wood's sad story was that he was, in the language of the day, queer—and, it was whispered, in love with a married Scoutmaster from Southall. His experiments with Brasso had placed him at death's door. He was taken away by civilian ambulance, covered in a blanket.

In our lot, as we spoke of the unselected rabble who slept and ate together, there were people like myself who had just finished a sixth-form course and others who were strangers to the written word, including Tony, Ronnie the Burglar and Fat Mick, who owned and raced greyhounds under his father's name. In these underlit and ghost-haunted barracks I met my first public school boy, an earnest big-ears called Henry, and my first real psychopath, a highly troubled Londoner by the name of Puckworth.

We marched; we saluted; we learned never to speak until spoken to. The drill sergeant was an old sweat with a ruined nose and watery eyes. In the time-honoured traditions of his calling, he swore on his mother's grave that we were the worst recruits he had ever been lumbered with.

'Even the bleedin' gyppos would send you home in disgrace, you horrible bunch of pox-doctors' clerks. Puckworth, I seen lampposts in the street with more feeling for left and right than what you have got.'

'Garn, piss off,' Puckworth replied. Somehow his head had shrunk since being issued with its beret, so that he stood in the ranks like a circus clown, vexed and ill-tempered. Sergeant Morris raised his eyes to a weeping heaven. His arms swept up in urgent semaphore.

'Tell me I never heard that, O Lord. Tell me I am dreaming.'

After lights-out bedsprings twanged as thirty or so squaddies masturbated gloomily. Some did it in despair (I supposed) and some to exhibit an anarchical freedom over bodies that were otherwise the annexed property of Her Majesty the Queen. Some because it was their nightly ritual; some because the susurration and mingled groans were in themselves highly erotic.

'Ouf!' Puckworth yelped at the other end of the room.

'Take that!'

It was the genius of the army to have placed the public school boy Henry, in the next bed.

'Your sister's a very lucky girl, Puckers,' he drawled in the dark, forcing a shout of laughter from the rest of us that brought Lance Corporal Denison racing out from his cubbyhole.

On the fourth day, we were summoned one by one to take a Basic Aptitude Test, held in a small office and invigilated over by a dusty-looking captain with an air of such general unhappiness as to wring the heart. He laid out the tools of his trade on a green baize cloth.

'Now, in this box I have an object that I want you to take to pieces down to its last component and then reassemble. I shall time you with this stopwatch. You will begin on my word of command. Have you understood the instructions?'

'Yessir,' I said, not without dread. I was imagining some arcane piece of military equipment, or possibly something familiar but dangerous, like a loaded revolver. The captain fiddled about, experimenting with the stopwatch buttons. Tension mounted.

'Go!' he shouted suddenly.

Inside the box was a bicycle lamp.

'That was quick,' the captain said when I had finished. He searched his papers for an explanation. 'Ah, yes. I note that you have only just left school.'

'Yessir. But my grandparents had a bicycle repair shop and that helped.'

'And you? Do you think you could lead men? Are you a natural leader?'

'I shouldn't think so.'

This disappointed him. He stared at the time it had taken me to play with the bicycle lamp, a result he had scribbled down on a scrap of feint-ruled paper.

'Let me give you a piece of advice. Next time someone asks you a question about leadership, say you think of little else. Otherwise you'll be pushing swill buckets about for two years of your life. I suppose you're going to university?'

'I haven't applied anywhere.'

We sat in silence for a few moments, the captain plucking gloomily at his nose with a thumb and forefinger. Both of us were thinking about college scarves and muffins toasted on gas fires, guileless girls with their legs tucked up under them on rackety chintz sofas. Behind them the door to the bedroom was open.

In the end, six of the intake were issued rail warrants and told to attend Officer Pre-Selection in Bury St Edmunds. As a subtle punishment for being educated beyond the true needs of the army, we were also ordered to take with us on the journey a huge mound of boots, tied together by their laces and with their owners' identities written on cardboard tickets. When we asked for a truck to the station, it raised a hollow laugh.

'There's six of you,' the guard commander pointed out. 'And you can always get a few grannies to help if the going gets tough. Now don't you go losing them boots. They're on their way to Korea, once some real soldiers have got their feet in them.'

The epic passage of these boots from Bedford to Bury St Edmunds was eased on the first part of the journey because the train to Cambridge had a guard's van, where we sat tying the loose ones back on to the heap, our heads hanging low in shame. Nobody with such a fretful parcel, about the size of two armchairs, should also have had the ignominy of having to ask directions to the station. It was that period of our island's history when it was thought richly comic to shout at squaddies, 'Thank God we've got a navy,' a taunt we heard several times. Helpful old biddies stopped to point as we ran back for the stray boots, soon numbered in dozens. Four of us to drag the main pile, two to follow after with armfuls of unmatched footwear. The pavement behind us was littered with little squares of cardboard.

At Cambridge, though things had gone badly, we felt half our troubles were over. We ate the huge and fluffy cheese sandwiches provided by the cookhouse and drank mugs of tea from the station buffet. Henry, the public school boy, was our unofficial leader, not because he was especially resourceful but rather that he was the first to propose that, whatever happened, we could not be blamed for doing our best. He repeated this so often that it finally became clear to everyone that blame was heading our way like a gale of frogs. We lay against the boots, smoking and worrying.

When the connection to Bury St Edmunds arrived, we found to our horror that it had no guard's van and, much worse, it was a corridor train. A surprising number of people were already seated as we turned the pyramid of boots into a ramshackle leather wall, waist high, which we fed into the corridor with only seconds to spare before the train moved off. At every stop, we had to shuffle the boots this way and that to allow passengers to alight. The ticket guard was incensed. Henry explained.

'These boots are going to men who will soon be fighting for your freedom. Accordingly, they must get through.'

'I never seen nothing like it in all my life,' the guard bellowed.

'Neither have I,' Henry admitted. 'But there you are.'

It was dusk when we reached Bury St Edmunds and a sharp rain was falling. A kindly porter, who identified himself as a former lance-jack in the Royal Electrical and Mechanical Engineers, suggested ringing Gibraltar Barracks and demanding—not requesting, demanding—transport. Henry followed him into a hut on the station and was gone some while. When he came out, he looked ashen under the sputtering gas lamps.

'It isn't far, apparently, and quite easy to find.'

We began rolling the boots like a snowball down the glistening wet pavements, jeered by incredulous crowds on their way to a boxing match in the town centre. Our morale was low, to the point where we kicked along the boots that had broken free, like sulky schoolboys. We reached the barracks drenched to the skin. A slitty-eyed corporal of the guard emerged from the gatehouse.

'It's a joke, ennit? Some kind of bleedin' joke. Straighten yourselves up. Tie them loose boots back on. Put your berets on straight and tuck them trousers back into them gaiters—'

He stopped to snap a salute at the officer of the day ambling round the corner, a young subaltern with an unfriendly moustache.

'Who are these horrible soldiers, Cor' Tanner?'

'Well, sir—'

'Horrible or not, we've brought your bloody boots from Bedford,' Henry interrupted, matching the lieutenant drawl for drawl.

He was immediately charged with insubordination and failing to address an officer in the correct manner. The rain lashed down on us all and there was a great deal of shouting and carrying on. We at least had been expected, but the boots not. Things were worse than that, even. These boots, in all their disarray, had technically ceased to exist—we had accidentally left the manifest or movement order or whatever (a smudged sheet of woolly paper) on the train. Though they were staring us in the face and filling with rain, on paper they had no being.

Gibraltar Barracks was the depot of the Suffolk Regiment. The barrack houses were nineteenth century and the ablution blocks dated from the recent war, though in the officers' mess there was silver going back to a much earlier age. The Suffolks were a proud bunch and liked a bit of swank with their soldiering. The drill sergeant, an impressive figure who would have done well defending Rorke's Drift from the Zulus, was the superbly named Sergeant Holyoake. Mustered on the foggy parade ground, we would hear him long before we could see him, his heels cracking out a tattoo on the sanded tarmac. Holyoake had a genuine gift for humour.

'I had tinned tomatoes with my sausage this morning. That is horrible food. That is runny and—here is my word for it— disappointing. That don't look like no effing tomato I ever seen. No matter, says I to Sergeant Cleaver. I will curb my disappointment. I have my boys to look forward to.'

His voice rose to a roar.

'Only to come on here and see men—grown men—make them tinned tomatoes look like effing works of art. Make them look like effing horticultural gods!'

We potential officers were grouped together in one squad of thirty men, drawn from three regiments. Unfortunately for all of us, we had a real madman in our midst. He began modestly by scraping the design from the lid of his tin of Cherry Blossom and polishing the raw metal. Soon enough, we all had to do it. Then he found that the iron frame of his bed would receive boot blacking and we were all forced to do this too. The floor drew his attention next and we bleached the pine boards white with soap powder. This left the nail heads looking shabby until this man—who was destined to be an officer and so in theory lead men into battle against heartless Russians—hit on the expedient of polishing them with Brasso. We were so much in the grip of hysteria that, on the occasion of one inspection, we cleaned the room, made up our beds (walking about in socks the while) and agreed to sleep in the lavatory.

There was one problem: Henry, gangling, muddled and—as far as bullshit was concerned—ineducable. The madman hit on an idea, and if it seems absurd now, at the time it made good sense. Henry's bed, locker, equipment and everything else were posted through a hatch in the ceiling and the remaining beds artfully arranged to conceal the gap. After breakfast, still in his pyjamas, he was likewise boosted into the roofspace. Like the boots from Bedford, he had temporarily ceased to exist.

We would have got away with it, until the moment when, alone in the dark, Henry missed his footing and plunged one pyjama-ed leg through the barracks ceiling, showering the adjutant and Sergeant Holyoake with plaster. The ghost of Hamlet's father never made a more dramatic appearance, nor uttered such a feeble entrance line.

'Sorry about that,' he called out indistinctly. 'Bloody miserable up here.'

The madman's hash was settled by an inter-platoon boxing tournament, in which the potential officer cadets were matched with the regular Suffolk intake, weight for weight, irrespective of experience. At the time I weighed ten stone four pounds, and the only boxing I had done was being banged about in the back garden by my father. I searched out my opponent, whose ten stone four was distributed very differently. He was a farm boy barely five feet six tall. Bribery was useless; he was going to kill me.

'Rubbish,' the madman in our ranks snapped. 'Boxing's a science.'

I fought the bout immediately after his, getting into a ring slippery with blood and snot. He himself was in an ambulance, on the way to hospital with a fractured jaw. I didn't fare much better.

The place where I had tried to bribe my opponent was the NAAFI hut, in which pleasure was measured out in pennies: tea, a butterless scone, on pay day ten Woodies or a half-ounce block of Golden Virginia. One night, I sat down with a bit of their headed notepaper and wrote to Trinity College, Cambridge, brushing crumbs of Bakewell tart from the text. Of Trinity, I knew only that it was a big college. My story was brief. Trinity had never heard of me but I had things to offer that might interest them: desire, ambition, devotion to scholarship, a full heart. I sealed the envelope without knowing that very few students of English were admitted there.

I received a laconic reply, saying that never before had the author received a letter from the NAAFI, that the grades I had mentioned were most impressive (my first experience of timeless academic sarcasm) and that he greatly regretted that my present situation made an interview (or so he must suppose) difficult to arrange. I read so far with blushing embarrassment, only to choke on the last sentence. In light of the circumstances, therefore, he would waive normal procedures and was pleased to offer me a place in October 1955.

I showed this amazing letter to Henry, who suggested I write a carefully nonchalant word of thanks that nevertheless incorporated a subtle reiteration of the offer and confirmation that I accepted it.

'Maybe you should keep the NAAFI notepaper thing going one more time when you reply. But make it clear that, after that, all future correspondence should be sent to your people at home.'

'My people?'

'Your parents,' he amended, colouring slightly.

His days with us were numbered. Falling through the barrack-room ceiling had convinced the CO that Henry was not the sort of man who would make an outstanding junior subaltern of infantry on any battlefield, nuclear or not. Knocking out his opponent in the first round at the boxing tournament proved no mitigation of circumstance, either. He had hit Private Ball a millisecond after the bell for the first round, while Ball was still adjusting the waistband of his PT shorts. It was held—even by us—an unsporting thing to do. Henry, with his genial drawl and jug ears, his Peterson pipe and all his many anecdotes of the daily round in rural Norfolk, was being posted to the Intelligence Corps.

'I think I am supposed to feel ashamed,' he explained.

'But you don't.'

'Hardly. A change of scene is always welcome. And, taking a wider view, it's no bad thing to put blokes who can't stand the army into Intelligence. You don't want ambitious or energetic people messing things up. Short wars, that's the answer. Office hours and short wars.'

'Are you going to university, Henry?'

'I suppose I could,' he mused, not without a sly smile. 'Though look at the people they're letting in these days.' He patted me on the shoulder. 'Only joking.'

That was the thing of it: I did consider myself an impostor. My native accent was still unreconstructed lower-middle-class London, as compared to Henry's burbling received pronunciation. He had been to places I knew nothing about, even though they existed in my own country. There was an uncle in Northumberland, for example, and not one but two aunts on the Isle of Wight. He owned things I had never before seen, such as monogrammed silver hairbrushes and a dark blue sponge bag that actually contained a sponge. He was, I considered, the real article.

'But then,' he objected, 'you are so amazingly anxious about everything that you'll go to university and do well and end up running the country.'

'You see me as anxious?'

'Twitchy.'

He thought about it some more, filling his Peterson with tobacco sent from home and lighting it with a luxurious flourish from an ancient brass lighter.

'Uncertain,' he settled on finally.

I wrote to my mother, telling her that whatever she did, she must keep any letter from Trinity safe and not bin it, or use it to light the boiler. Under no circumstances was she to show the envelope to my father. On the other hand, she could tell him that I was going before a War Office Selection Board in February, with a view to becoming an officer. Indeed, she could make of that as much as she liked.

There was leave at Christmas and I hitched home by various indirections, clumping up Eastfield Road in my ammunition boots, the greatcoat I was wearing heavy with rain. My father opened the door and studied me through a cloud of Capstan Full Strength. His first words were utterly predictable.

'Thank God we've got a navy.'

My mother had hidden the letter from Trinity in a saucepan and I recovered it during the first cup of tea we took alone.

'What does it mean?' she asked.

'I've got a place there to read English.'

'What I'm saying is: who's going to pay?'

'The British taxpayer.'

'Ha!' she snorted. 'I can see the kind of people you've been hanging out with. And your father's none too pleased about this officer business you told me to tell him about. He doesn't think you'll ever be an officer.'

'Tell him he can get knotted.'

'You tell him. He'll like that.'

But in the end it wasn't the idea of me becoming an officer that distressed him but the offer from Trinity. Many years later, somebody wiser than me pointed out that he was a constitutionally jealous person. I suggested a better word might be envious, but the word jealousy carries with it a sexual charge that reflected his own history. Regarding university, I had in some way given myself to a secret lover, someone he would never meet.

'What does it tell you that you got in just by writing some silly scruffy letter?' he huffed. 'It tells me something.'

'And what's that?'

'They are having trouble making up the numbers.'

However, mentioning it around the office next day changed his mind a little. His colleagues were very impressed by Trinity's generosity. He came home with a different take.

'Of course, it's one of the biggest colleges, measured in numbers of students. That helped.'

'Yesterday you said they were making up the numbers.'

'I've got better things to think about,' he said, ending the argument.

My girlfriend and her parents took a much more positive view of the way things had turned out in three short months. Her father had never come across the Suffolks on his march to the Rhine but knew people who spoke well of them. Wise bird that he was, he had also met enough childlike wartime subalterns to recognize the type in me.

'If they want to make you an officer,' he explained, 'you don't really have a lot of say in the matter. I should think you'll do very well, what with being tall and that.'

He was unconsciously echoing the sentiments of my Uncle Jim. The night before I joined the army my father had taken me to Kentish Town to see his brother. Four pints and a couple of whiskies had seen me legless, throwing up into a garden hedge along the Seven Sisters Road.

'I think you're going to make a lovely little soldier,' Jim said, cradling my spinning head. 'You've got the hang of it already. Once you've got your knees brown, there'll be no stopping you.'

'Let me die,' I moaned.

'That comes later,' he said.

The War Office Selection Board was a four-day affair that concentrated on skills of a kind not often employed in anything resembling the world of real events. Split into teams, we attempted to bridge muddy pits with a forty-gallon oil drum, a few bits of wood and unequal lengths of scaffolding pole. One frosty morning, in an individual test, we climbed to the top of a very tall tree and leaped for a rope dangling an enticing four or five feet away. Some candidates refused. When this happened, the officer sitting on a trembling bough nearby made furtive notes on his clipboard.

'Bad luck,' he said diplomatically.

To demonstrate the quality of mind required in a junior officer, we delivered lectures to each other on a variety of subjects that might attract the attention of the examiners. I remember one candidate gave a compelling account of the social history of whisky, which was much praised by a conducting officer with a face ravaged by his own research into the topic.

At the end of the course there was a one-on-one interview. I was shown into the presence of a major with a silly-ass moustache and a generous row of campaign medals. Whether he had ever found cause to jump out of a tree to clutch at a rope seemed doubtful; he was where he was because of a minor public school education and job vacancies created by the fortunes of war. A practised suavity filled his side of the desk.

'Know anything about wine?' he asked as his first question.

'Never drunk it, sir.'

'What's your favourite grub?'

'Shepherd's pie.'

'Good man,' he said admiringly. 'Cook it yourself, can you?'

There was a potential trap here: if I said yes, he might well ask whether I enjoyed needlepoint or had a boyfriend who played the violin. I temporized.

'It's the only thing I can cook.'

'Lucky blighter. The best shepherd's pie I ever ate was in Cairo.'

I waited for the punchline; there wasn't one. He drew a sheet of paper towards him.

'We'll just knock off these pro-forma questions. Has any member of your family ever held the Queen's Commission?'

'My father.'

'Good show,' he said, making a notation. 'Regiment?'

'The RAF.'

Sorrowfully, he scratched out what he had just written. We tried another tack.

'Rugby man?'

'Yes.'

'Greatest fly-half in the world today?'

'Jackie Kyle.'

'Getting a bit elderly, isn't he?'

'Genius is ageless.'

He smiled and wrote vigorously for a few moments.

I passed these tests (though only those who fell out of the tree or lectured on the iron truths of Leninist–Stalinist philosophy, Diaghilev or Doris Day ever failed) and spent sixteen weeks on the Duke of Westminster's estate as an officer cadet. Just before being commissioned, I was invited to nominate the regiment of my choice. My first pick was the Royal Fusiliers, a sign of complete social ignorance that was treated as such. The second was the Somaliland Scouts and the third the King's African Rifles.

Newly commissioned officers had a clothing allowance of £74, with which they were supposed to buy patrols—mess uniform—and whatever other little outward signs of rank they fancied. My father got me to sign this draft over to him; my mother went off to jumble sales to find a dinner jacket as a replacement. She came home with something that the great cornet player Bix Beiderbecke might have worn when playing hotel gigs in New Orleans thirty years earlier. Modelling it, I looked like a walk-on in some provincial rep.

'I am trying to make a good impression,' I wailed.

'Not everybody can look like George Raft.'

'I don't want to look like George Raft either.'

'You'll get used to it,' she sighed.

My girlfriend and I spent our last evening together for sixteen months going to see the film *Gigi* in Leicester Square and then walking to Goodge Street, where coaches were waiting to take about 120 of us to Northolt, whence we would fly to Kenya, a country I had barely heard of in a continent of which I knew nothing.

'You'll write?' she asked.

'Every day,' I promised. □

STATEMENT OF OWNERSHIP, MANAGEMENT, AND CIRCULATION
1. Publication Title: Granta
2. Publication No.: 0000-508
3. Filing Date: 27 September 2006
4. Issue Frequency: Quarterly (4 times per year)
5. Number of Issues Published Annually: 4
6. Annual Subscription Price: $39.95
7. Complete Mailing Address of Known Office of Publication: 841 Broadway, New York, NY 10003-4793
8. Complete Mailing Address of Headquarters of General Business Office of Publisher: 841 Broadway, New York, NY 10003-4793
9. Full Names and Complete Mailing Addresses of Publisher, Editor, and Managing Editor: Publisher: Sigrid Rausing, 2/3 Hanover Yard, Noel Road, London, N1 8BE, UK; Editor: Ian Jack, 2/3 Hanover Yard, Noel Road, London N1 8BE, UK; Managing Editor: Fatema Ahmed, 2/3 Hanover Yard, Noel Road, London N1 8BE, UK
10. Owner: Sigrid Rausing, Eardley House, 4 Uxbridge Street, London, W8 7SY, UK
11. Known Bondholders, Mortgagees, and Other Security Holders: None
12. Tax Status: Has Not Changed
13. Publication Title: Granta
14. Issue Date for Circulation Data: Summer 2006
15. Extent and Nature of Circulation: Average No. Copies Each Issue During Preceding 12 Months:
a. Total No. of Copies: 27,027
b. Paid and/or Requested Circulation:
1. Paid/Requested Outside-County Mail Subscriptions Stated on Form 3541: 14,471
2. Paid In-County Subscriptions Stated on Form 3541: 0
3. Sales Through Dealers and Carriers, Street Vendors, Counter Sales and Other Non-USPS Paid Distribution: 3,338
4. Other Classes Mailed Through the USPS: 0
c. Total Paid and/or Requested Circulation: 17,809
d. Free Distribution by Mail:
1. Outside-County as Stated on Form 3541: 0
2. In-County as Stated on Form 3541: 0
3. Other Classes Mailed Through the USPS: 221
e. Free Distribution Outside the Mail: 0
f. Total Free Distribution: 221
g. Total Distribution: 18,030
h. Copies not Distributed: 8,997
i. Total: 27,027
j. Percent Paid and/or Requested Circulation: 98.8%
Extent and Nature of Circulation: No. Copies of Single Issue Published Nearest to Filing Date:
a. Total No. of Copies: 22,092
b. Paid and/or Requested Circulation:
1. Paid/Requested Outside-County Mail Subscriptions Stated on Form 3541: 12,786
2. Paid In-County Subscriptions Stated on Form 3541: 0
3. Sales Through Dealers and Carriers, Street Vendors, Counter Sales and Other Non-USPS Paid Distribution: 3,264
4. Other Classes Mailed Through the USPS: 0
c. Total Paid and/or Requested Circulation: 16,050
d. Free Distribution by Mail:
1. Outside-County as Stated on Form 3541: 0
2. In-County as Stated on Form 3541: 0
3. Other Classes Mailed Through the USPS: 192
e. Free Distribution Outside the Mail: 0
f. Total Free Distribution: 192
g. Total Distribution: 16,242
h. Copies not Distributed: 5,850
i. Total: 22,092
j. Percent Paid and/or Requested Circulation: 98.8%
16. Publication of Statement of Ownership will be printed in the Winter 2006 issue of this publication.
17. Signature and Title of Editor, Publisher, Business Manager, or Owner: I certify that all information furnished on this form is true and complete. Ian Jack, Editor

GRANTA

LIKE AN EPISODE
OF *L.A. LAW*

A. M. Homes

Deposition—a curious word meaning to remove from office or a position of power and/or testimony under oath—a written statement by a witness for use in court in his absence.

Deposition: I think of suing my father to prove that he is my father and just the phrasing—suing my father to prove that he is my father—has the equally surreal echo of the moment my mother told me that my mother was dead.

I am adopted—I grew up knowing that I was the mistress's daughter, that my mother had been young and unmarried and my father was older and married with a family of his own. In 1992 my biological parents resurfaced, and at my first meeting with my father he proposed the idea of a DNA test, saying that his wife wanted and needed him to prove that I was his child and that it would allow him to take me into his family.

The entire episode was sufficiently strange that it seemed smart to apply a bit of science, to bring fact into a situation that was otherwise entirely emotional and almost pathological in its peculiarity.

My father and I had our blood drawn, several months passed and my father called to tell me he had the results. 'The test says it's 99.9 per cent likely I'm your father,' he said. 'So what are my responsibilities?'

I said nothing. There was nothing to say.

He never managed to take me into his family; his other children found out about my existence only accidentally—after a letter I'd sent to my father was opened by mistake by his youngest son.

I never asked for a copy of the DNA test—never questioned it—and my relationship to my biological parents ended rather abruptly; in 1998 my biological mother died at sixty years old, alone on her sofa in Atlantic City, New Jersey. My biological father knew she was ill; she had asked him to speak to me about donating a kidney and he refused, saying they couldn't ask me for anything considering how they'd never done anything for me. My father and I had one final conversation after my mother died. I told him that I'd had enough, that I couldn't do this again—that I didn't want to one day get a call summoning me to another church, where I'd stand in the back, unwelcome, and witness friends and family mourning the passing of a man I never really knew but was somehow a part of.

'I understand,' he said. 'Call me. Call me in the car. My wife isn't in the car very often—we can talk.'

'I'm not your mistress. I'm your daughter. And I'm not calling you in your car,' I said.

'Fine thing,' he replied.

Several years later, as part of a quest to know more about my background, I asked a lawyer to call my father and request a copy of the DNA test. Naively I assumed he would provide it. My father refused. I had the lawyer ask again, pointing out that legally I was most likely entitled to the information. My father again refused and this time asked the lawyer not to call him any more. I brought in more lawyers, who together pondered what might be done to compel my father to produce the document; could we sue for paternity, for breach of contract, unfair use of the results?

Suing my father—I picture the papers being filed, a summons served telling him to appear at a certain place at a certain time. I imagine there being a man, a stranger to both of us, someone hired to do the job, to ask the questions.

Mr Hecht, before we begin I would like to remind you that the length of a deposition is limited to seven hours a day, over the course of however many days it takes to do the kind of call and response, asking of questions related to the actions and activities of the last forty-four years—that's how old she is now, the infant in question.

Rules of Civil Procedure. Rule 26—Discovery. We will be asking you, the deposed, to provide a copy of your birth certificate and a copy of the DNA test which you and Ms Homes jointly participated in. Given that a potential witness is anyone who has information relevant to the issues of a lawsuit or who has information that may lead to relevant information, we will also call your wife and your children. Unlike a trial, where a judge can rule on objections, at a deposition lawyers can ask irrelevant questions and enquire into hearsay.

Is all of this clear?

Have you ever had your deposition taken before?

Do you understand that you are under oath—sworn to tell the truth?

Are you prepared to answer my questions?

Is there anything about your physical state—are you taking any medications that will prevent you from giving me complete and truthful answers?

If you need to take a break at any time, let me know.

What is your full name?

Your place and date of birth?

Your parents' names and place and date of birth?

Mr Hecht, can you tell me why are we here today? Is there a particular issue?

In 1993 you asked Ms Homes to participate in a DNA blood test which would genetically compare DNA samples from both you and Ms Homes to prove that in fact you are her father. And the result of that test showed that it was 99.9 per cent likely that you are her father, and recently when she requested a copy of that test from you, you declined to provide it—is that correct?

You asked Ms Homes to participate in the test, but you don't believe you should both have access to the results.

Why is that?

You participated equally?

You paid for the test, Mr Hecht—actually you had some trouble paying for the test, didn't you? You scheduled the appointment for the test in July of 1993, Ms Homes travelled from New York to Washington and met you at the lab, but you didn't have the right kind of payment, the right kind of cheque—and you had to go back again the next day?

At the time you scheduled the test, Ms Homes offered to pay for the test as well or split the cost with you?

Now, if it is all about the money—the costs associated with this meeting here today are in excess of the charges for the test. So perhaps this is not about money?

How would you describe yourself, Mr Hecht?

Would you describe yourself as a family man?

Is there more to you than that—than just a retired businessman?

Are you close to your family?

Do you go to church?

You have a son and a nephew who share your name—what does the name mean to you?

What is your identity, Mr Hecht?

Did you always know who you were?

Have you ever been arrested?

Been charged with a crime?

For the record, can you tell us about any and all claims, lawsuits that you've been involved in over the years?

What was your age and place of first employment?

And your last—were you fired or asked to step down?

Did you feel any personal responsibility?

Do you think of yourself as someone who gets things done?

Has anyone ever called you a big shot?

Do you think you're an average man?

Same level of ambition as your peers?

Did you graduate from college?

Were you in the army? Ever kill anyone?

Where did you grow up, Mr Hecht?

How would you describe your childhood?

Who raised you?

How was it that you lived with your grandparents—where were your mother and father?

How did your parents meet?

What did your father do for a living?

How would you describe your relationship with your father?

Were you close?

Did he love you?

Do you think it's true that boys are closer to their mothers and girls to their fathers?

Are you proud of your family history?

Involved in any lineage organizations?

What clubs are you a member of?

Have you ever wanted to join a club and not been allowed in?

What kind of name is Hecht?

A. M. Homes

Was your father Jewish?
Was he raised in a Jewish home?
Did your mother's family consider you Jewish?
Was your father's father a kosher butcher?
Why did your paternal grandmother carry a gun?

Would you describe yourself as charitable?
Do you give money to charities?
Do you give of your time and abilities?
Do you drink?
Did you ever use recreational drugs?
Ever smoke marijuana?
Ever take pills for energy?
Ever use cocaine?
Ever try Viagra?

Where did you meet your wife?
At what age were you married?
Did you engage in relations before the wedding?
Was she a virgin?
Were *you*?
Have you ever had a sexually transmitted disease?

When did you last have sex, Mr Hecht?
With whom?
Would you say that you and your wife had a good sex life?
Did you and your wife ever discuss open marriage?
So, initially she didn't know that you were having a sexual
relationship with Ms Ballman?
Was Ms Ballman your first relationship outside of your marriage,
or did someone precede her?

How did your wife find out about Ms Ballman?
Can you tell me the names of your children?
Do you know their birth dates?
Besides Ms Homes—did you have any other children outside of
your marriage?
Is it possible, Mr Hecht, that there are others?

How many relationships did you have outside your marriage?
How long did they last?
Your wife was pregnant at the same time as Ms Ballman?

How old was Ms Ballman when you met her?
How would you describe her physically—her appearance?
Did you know that she was a minor?
What were the circumstances of that meeting?
Were you the owner of the Princess Shop?
How long did Ms Ballman work for you?
When did your sexual relationship begin?
What were the circumstances of that first encounter?
Was she a virgin?
Do you think your libido is average?
Was Ms Ballman a nymphomaniac?
Was she a lesbian?
Did you once tell Ms Homes that Ellen Ballman was a nymphomaniac and on another occasion that she was a lesbian?
Did your male friends also have girls on the side?
How many of them knew Ms Ballman?
Did you worry that Ms Ballman was sleeping with other men—your friends?
When your sexual relationship with Ms Ballman began how old was she?
What would prompt a teenage girl in the 1950s to leave her mother's good care and take up with a married man?
Did Ellen Ballman tell you that someone was molesting her?
You told Ms Homes that Ms Ballman told you something that would have indicated that something was happening in her mother's home and that you probably should have listened better.
Did you take advantage of Ms Ballman?
Did you use birth control?

Did Ms Ballman meet your family—your mother?
Your children?
Your wife?
How did it happen that your eldest son spent time with Ms Ballman?

A. M. Homes

When did you realize you were in love with Ms Ballman?
So, were you or were you not in love with Ms Ballman?
Did she believe you were in love with her?
On more than one occasion did you propose marriage?
Even though you were already married, Mr Hecht, you proposed
to Ms Ballman when she was seventeen—you called her mother and
asked for permission to marry her?
How did you think you would explain that to your wife?
Do you believe in polygamy, Mr Hecht?
How and when did your wife find out that you and Ms Ballman
were having a relationship?
Did your wife know how old Ms Ballman was?
And what did you say to your wife? Again, I'd like to remind you
that you are under oath and your wife will be answering the same
question?

Did your wife contemplate divorcing you?
Is divorce in opposition to her faith?
Are you and your wife of the same faith?
Is adultery in opposition to your faith?
Are you a religious man, Mr Hecht?
Do you believe in heaven, Mr Hecht?

What was your nickname for Ms Ballman?
Was 'the Dragon Lady' one of them?
Where did that come from? Was it from something you shared?
Did Ms Ballman have you arrested for deserting her?
When Ms Ballman was pregnant you sent her to Florida to live
and said you'd be joining her there—but you never showed up?
And your wife was pregnant at the same time as Ms Ballman?
You must have felt like an exceptionally fertile man?

Later in the pregnancy did you visit Ms Ballman at her mother's
home?
Did you offer to take her shopping to buy things for the baby?
Did you have Ms Ballman meet with you and your lawyer and
together discuss the fact that 'there are only so many slices of the
pie?'

Did you ask either Ms Ballman or your wife to consider an abortion?

Can you swim, Mr Hecht?

I'm just wondering if at some point during all this you felt like you were going under. Drowning.

When was the last time you saw Ms Ballman pregnant? What month was that?

How did you hear about the birth of your child with Ms Ballman?

Were you ever asked to sign any legal documents relating to the child?

How long did your relationship with Ms Ballman last?

Did Ms Ballman ever marry?

Are you proud of your daughter, Mr Hecht?

Are you proud of Ms Homes?

Have you read her work?

Did you ask your daughter to meet you in hotels?

Why not coffee shops?

What is the nature of your thoughts about your daughter?

Did your wife know when and where you were meeting your daughter?

If you had been meeting one of your other children, would she have known?

Are you circumcised?

Is this common knowledge?

Does your other daughter know?

Why was this information that you shared with Ms Homes?

How did your other children find out that they had a sister?

And what was their reaction to discovering that information?

Do you think of yourself as a good father?

Let's backtrack a little bit...

In May of 1993 you read a review of Ms Homes's book in the *Washington Post* and called her in New York City?

What prompted you to call her on that day?

If Ms Homes were not a successful, well-known figure, would you have ever called her?

You made a plan to meet in Washington several days later?

Was anyone else at the meeting? Was the meeting taped or otherwise recorded or monitored by anyone?

What was your reaction to meeting Ms Homes?

When you met her were you surprised by the degree to which she looks like you?

Does she look more like you than your other children?

Despite the physical similarity at that meeting you asked Ms Homes if she would consent to a paternity test—saying that you had no question as to the likelihood that she was your child, but that your wife was insisting, and that you would need that in order to be able to take her into your famil. Is that correct?

What made you question Ms Homes's paternity?

After the blood was drawn, as you were walking out with Ms Homes you told her you had something you wanted to give her—and yet you didn't give her anything?

What did you want to give her?

Was it something of your mother's? A family heirloom?

Several months later, you phoned Ms Homes to say you had the results of the test, and you asked Ms Homes to once again meet you in a hotel in Maryland?

At that meeting you told Ms Homes that you were in fact her father—that the DNA test said it was 99.9 per cent likely—and you asked, 'What are my responsibilities?'

What did you envision as your responsibilities?

What were your intentions towards Ms Homes when you asked her to submit to the test?

Did you follow through by 'taking her into your family?'

Before you discussed the results with Ms Homes, did you discuss them with anyone else?

Did you discuss them with your wife?

Why did you not offer Ms Homes a copy of the test result?

What did you do with the test result?

When did you give a copy to your lawyer?

Did you keep a copy for yourself?

Do you typically give the one and only copy of an important document to your attorney?

Did you not put it in your safe deposit box because you didn't want your wife to discover it?

But didn't you tell Ms Homes that it was your wife who insisted on Ms Homes having the paternity test before you could 'take her into your family'?

Was the reason your wife wanted Ms Homes to have the DNA test because you had portrayed Ms Ballman to your wife as a floozy to make it seem like you were Ms Ballman's victim?

You arranged for your eldest son to meet Ms Homes?

How did that meeting go?

Was your son happy to have more information about something that had only been a dim memory from his childhood—the time he spent with Ms Ballman?

Was there a lot of tension in your home when your eldest son was a boy?

What was the occasion of your wife meeting Ms Homes?

Is there a reason why your wife wouldn't like Ms Homes?

Why did you say to Ms Homes later that she and your wife didn't hit it off?

Did Ms Homes ever ask you for anything?

Do you have concerns about Ms Homes making a claim on your estate?

Did she ever in any way indicate that she had any interest in your estate?

Did you have her take the paternity test in order that you might by name exclude her from your estate?

When did you last speak to Ms Ballman?

And what was the substance of that call?

Did you see Ms Ballman in the months before she died?

Did your wife know you were meeting her?

How did she look? Was she still attractive?

Did Ms Ballman ask you to ask Ms Homes if she would give her a kidney?

And what did you tell Ms Ballman?

Did you later tell Ms Ballman that in fact you had asked Ms Homes and that she said no?

Did it occur to you that this misinformation meant that Ms Homes did not know about Ms Ballman's condition, nor did she have a chance to say goodbye?

Did you go to your own personal doctor and enquire about donating a kidney to Ms Ballman?

Did you tell Ms Homes that you had done that?

And what would your wife have thought about that—would you have had the surgery without telling her?

Did you know that Ms Ballman was going to die?

How did you feel when you heard that Ms Ballman had passed?

And your last phone call with Ms Homes—several months after Ms Ballman's death—how did that go?

How did it end? Did you say, 'Call me anytime, call me in my car, my wife's not usually in the car'?

Why would Ms Homes need to call you in the car as opposed to in your home?

Is anyone harming you, confining you, not allowing you to make and receive calls and/or mail?

Are you angry with Ms Homes?

When Ms Homes's New York lawyer called you—the same man who called you to tell you that Ms Ballman had passed—and asked you for a copy of the DNA test, you told him never to call you again and referred him to your lawyer.

Mr Glick called your lawyer and was told by your lawyer that the DNA document had been misplaced and that you would not sign an affidavit of paternity.

Did you know that Mr Smith had misplaced the test results?

Are you concerned that other important documents may have been misplaced or mishandled?

Does it not seem a little too convenient that Ms Homes is asking for this document, and now it is missing?

You have children and now grandchildren? Do they look like you, Mr Hecht?

You have adopted grandchildren as well. Do they look like you also?

Do they have a right to know who they are—where they came from?

What is your understanding of why Ms Homes wants this document?

If Ms Homes is your biological relative, why should she not be treated in the same way that your other equally biological children are treated? Why should she have different, less than equal, rights?

Does that seem fair? Are you a fair man? A just man?

Could you please repeat for the record your name?

And Mr Hecht, could you please for the record state the names of all your children? □